The Definitive Guide
IT Service Metrics

The Definitive Guide to IT Service Metrics

KURT McWHIRTER

AND

TED GAUGHAN

IT Governance Publishing

IT Governance Publishing

IT Governance Limited

Unit 3, Clive Court

Bartholomew's Walk

Cambridgeshire Business Park

Ely

Cambridgeshire

CB7 4EA

United Kingdom

www.itgovernance.co.uk

First published in the United Kingdom in 2012
by IT Governance Publishing.

ISBN 978-1-84928-405-9

FOREWORD

Metrics. A word that strikes 'panic' in many service managers. It seems no matter where I travel or who I speak to, it is an area that is a constant question. 'What do I measure? How often? Do I just take the measures from ITIL® and use them – they are published, they must be right. Right? Right?' Inevitably, my response focuses on the practical, 'What is the goal? What hurts? What are you trying to change?' Until now, there really has not been a reference where the 'why measure this' question was answered.

Finally, *The Definitive Guide to IT Service Metrics* is a reference that is both common sense and practical. I think you'll find that the metrics included are useful and may not be so common. The strength of this volume rests in the justification and explanations for each metric. The formulas are simple (simple is good, simple is powerful...) which allows the service manager to manipulate and fit to their environment. The 'why' has a 'because.'

A word of caution — don't just jump to the metrics — read the opening chapters. The information provides the basis for the chosen metrics and how they are measured. Missing this will diminish the overall content and the full benefit will not be realized.

I'm honored to introduce the first volume of the Thought Leadership Series. It is a wonderful volume and sets the stage for many more to come.

Suzanne D. Van Hove, Ed.D., FSM®
CEO, SED-IT

PREFACE

This book is an invaluable addition to every IT professional's library. Metrics are an increasingly important tool for the management of organizations. All too often, a workforce jumps into action with a flurry of activities with no real thought as to what the outcomes need to be. The end result is a great deal of spending for no tangible service results. This book provides an excellent defense against spending for no gain in service. It provides insights to the proper design, implementation and utilization of IT service lifecycle process metrics as a means of monitoring and controlling IT service delivery. Of particular value is the incorporation of recommendations for applying metrics as operational performance decision support tools.

The authors have applied industry-standard frameworks to the design and implementation of IT Service Management (ITSM) metrics. Based on the ITIL® 2011 service lifecycle processes along with principles from ISO/IEC 20000 and the Project Management Body of Knowledge (PMBOK™), it is a guide to developing and using metrics as a means of monitoring and controlling the delivery of IT services. The book includes a wide variety of detailed metrics to enable quick and direct implementation. It also contains guidelines for developing customized metrics based on specialized needs of the business.

Toby R. Gouker, PhD, GSLC
Chancellor, SANS Technology Institute

Preface

With the right amount of effort and determination, anyone can achieve some degree of success. However, to understand the level and extent of that success we need to be able to measure both our efforts and the results in order to know whether we have met or exceeded goals and expectations. The key to this understanding is found within the measurements and metrics collected during execution.

Metrics are the source of valuable information for any organization and can provide an abundance of benefits including:

- Demonstrating organizational maturity
- Driving and changing the behavior of the organization and staff
- Discovering opportunities for improvement
- Justification for change and the cost of change.

Having the information provided by metrics will help develop the knowledge necessary to improve decision making throughout the organization. Without metrics, decision making can become dependent upon knowledgeable individuals or, even worse, based upon guess work.

In order for any metric to provide benefit, we must understand our goals and expectations for the metric rooted in the success of the process, service, or product we are measuring. The goal(s) will give purpose and meaning for each metric and will help to justify the collection of data for the metric. The expectations help us understand the targets we must achieve for success. For our metrics, these targets are the Acceptable Quality Levels (AQLs) defined for each metric. An AQL should be established by the requirements documented for the process, service, or product (whether business or technical). Depending on the level of maturity, some organizations can clearly define their AQLs while others may need to collect initial metrics to baseline and then set trending goals for improvement. We provide AQLs for many of the metrics documented in this book. These are based on experience and feedback but, for the most part, they are nothing more than guidelines. In the end, you must determine your AQLs for each metric

Now that we have explained our thoughts concerning metrics and how important they can be, we want to make sure that you understand that developing, collecting, and reporting metrics is not a quick and easy effort to accomplish. While there are several organizations across the globe that have mature metrics capabilities, many that are already on the metrics path, and quite a few that are just starting; we want to make sure that there is an understanding of the struggles involved with achieving metric maturity. The most difficult part of developing metrics is dealing with different parts of the organization and the people involved. Understand that everyone has an opinion and that they will voice their opinion at either the right time or place. This will take time, patience, and compromise to create effective metrics. Other difficulties include tools, funding, and unknown requirements. Eventually, you will get past the development stage and come to agreement on a good set of metrics. We wish nothing but the best on this journey or that you are at least able to maintain your sanity.

So, as you move forward ensure that measurements and metrics are an early activity within your lifecycle and instill a positive and proactive mindset for these metrics. This mindset will help change the way your organization develops and manages the services offered. Remember this:

Finding problems and issues is a good thing: discovering opportunities is a great thing.

Create that positive mindset and use this book as a reference to create metrics for your services and environment. Then use these metrics to find opportunities to improve.

ABOUT THE AUTHORS

Kurt McWhirter has over 30 years of experience in IT strategic planning, operations management, and enterprise process design and implementation. He holds a Master of Business Administration (MBA) from Bellarmine University. Kurt is certified as an ITIL® Expert and ISO/IEC 20000 Consultant. He is also an ITIL® Trainer accredited with EXIN® and APMG® for all ITIL® 2007/2011 courses. He is accomplished in IT functional requirements analysis, budget planning and forecasting, and service process design and implementation. He has created and led several process workshops with senior business and IT management teams that assisted clients to develop strategies and processes aligned to business requirements. Kurt is a recognized authority on using the ITIL® framework to focus on business requirements that deliver high quality solutions to customers.

Ted Gaughan has over 25 years of experience in business/technical strategic development, program/project management, and IT engineering and operations management. He holds a Master of Arts in Management and Supervision from Central Michigan University. He is a certified Project Management Professional (PMP®), Process Design Engineer (CPDE®), ITIL® Expert, ISO/IEC 20000 Consultant and TIPA® Lead Assessor. He has managed numerous large enterprise IT project portfolios, applying ITIL®-based processes to maximize the utility of delivered results. Ted is an authority on assessing IT service processes, and planning and implementing IT service improvements.

ACKNOWLEDGEMENTS

We are eternally grateful to Dr. Suzanne Van Hove for her expert counsel and tireless support in preparing this book. Her unparalleled subject matter expertise provided invaluable insights to ensure metric accuracy. Suzanne is a cherished colleague and friend.

Our sincere thanks to Dr. Toby Gouker for his unwavering support. As an accomplished educator and subject matter expert, Toby eagerly shared his knowledge in validating the Information Security Management (ISM) metrics. We are honored by his review of the book.

Special thanks to Sandy Kelly and for her editorial reviews and professional feedback.

We would also like to acknowledge the helpful suggestions received from the following reviewers: Lionel Seaw, principal consultant, Sapience Consulting Pte. Ltd., Chris Evans MBCS DPSM—ITSM specialist, and John Custy, managing consultant, DPSM TM, JPC Group.

Table of Contents

CHAPTER 1: INTRODUCTION

We know change is inevitable. However, in many cases we don't seem to be fully prepared for the change. This is becoming more apparent in the Information Technology (IT) industries and organizations as changes in cultures and the working environment seem to meet greater resistance. Changing our technologies is relatively easy due to the rapid nature of change in our hardware and software and our willingness to apply these changes to remain up to date. Therefore, change is commonplace in any technology field; or is it?

Managing the infrastructure, both hardware and software, in our technology-centric world has commoditized the technologies and the skills to implement and manage the technologies. What we are not doing well is managing the business side of our technologies; and it's here that we find resistance to change. Managing technologies from the business viewpoint requires that cultural change in our mindset, attitudes, and methodologies. Higher levels of structure and discipline must become commonplace within our organizations to manage change from both the technology perspective and, more importantly, the changing business perspective. This requires new ways of managing the environment to create a service-oriented culture which provides value to the business while giving true purpose to the IT organization. And yes, we know you've heard this before and that everyone understands this 'service' mindset. Yet, we still struggle to get there.

We see so many individuals pushing back and rejecting service provision as just a new fad in the industry which will fade away like so many others in the past; but is it really fading away? The reason and justification stems from what is perceived as additional workload and burden on an already busy work day. Finding the time to develop and document metrics, implement and manage the tools to measure, and finally creating reports and meeting with the business regularly is difficult and as such, these activities are prioritized last. Ironically, a great deal of our measurements already occur; we just need to collect the measurements and metrics that provide evidence of our service provision. For example, look at how many measurements we use while driving our cars; we have the speedometer, a tachometer (measuring the engine's rotation), gas gauge, temperature gauge, oil pressure gauge, and so on; all used to measure the quality of our driving experience. We can find this in our IT environments as well. We just need the structure and discipline to change the way we work to provide good service and report the metrics showing our success.

As organizations begin down the service path, one of the more challenging areas, and the reason for this book, is the development of measurements and metrics that demonstrate value to the business and customers. IT has always had the ability to measure technology and performance but now we are asking IT to measure service provision and value to the business. In essence, we must now use our metrics to tell a story. This story must tell how the service is meeting the needs of the business and demonstrating value to either the internal or external customers using the evidence from our measurement activities.

While all measurements and metrics should provide value to the organization, in many cases a single metric provides limited, but valuable, information concerning performance. We see the power of a metric unleashed when combined with other metrics to give context and provide a complete picture of performance (further discussed in *Chapter 2*). Utilizing multiple metrics provides a greater understanding of the situation at hand and improves decision making when determining what actions to take.

This book contains several defined metrics to help tell that story of success and prove the value proposition offered by IT or a service provider. We provide several attributes for each metric including:

- Metric ownership – both the process and the role
- Stakeholders – who uses the metric or receives value from the metric?
- Description – identifying the metric purpose and use
- Formula (when applicable) – basic formulas providing a starting point for measuring
- Acceptable Quality Level (AQL) – sets a target for the metric.

Our goal is not to have you use these metrics straight from this book but rather provoke thought and innovation in the creation and use of metrics to bring value to your organization and business. As you develop metrics for your organization, you will find many metrics can be used for multiple processes and services. The benefits found within these metrics offer opportunities to provide evidence of activities such as:

- Demonstrating service or process performance
- Trending metrics to understand both the past and possibly the future
- Justification for need or acquisition
- Establish baselines and comparing against the baseline
- Troubleshooting
- Improvement opportunities.

There are many other tasks and activities that will use these metrics to offer proof of actions taken or evidence of actions to take.

The metrics in this book can be used directly in your environment and can offer benefits to both the IT organization and the business. However, the innovation is found in developing and collecting measurements and then bringing multiple measurements or metrics together to tell the story of success based on factual evidence of execution.

We hope you find value in this book and share it with others. Enjoy!

CHAPTER 2: USING METRICS

There are many ways to utilize metrics and get value from them and no one method is the best. The methods used to develop and implement metrics should be adapted to fit your needs and situation. Developing, implementing, and managing metrics goes well beyond simply purchasing a monitoring tool and collecting measurements. From our standpoint, metrics help us understand:

- Customers and their behaviors
- Industries and how they work
- The current environment (e.g. resources, budgets, locations, etc.)
- The infrastructure supporting services
- The value of the services provided
- Cost-justification for the service (comparing cost of the service to the benefits gained).

Therefore, a methodical process/procedure is required to understand these concepts in a concise and accurate manner that either provides or illustrates benefits to stakeholder groups.

This chapter will review areas that are important to consider when applying metrics. Use the considerations in this chapter to build your own methodology for developing and using metrics.

Understanding metrics

Be prudent when choosing the measurements and metrics as this can become unmanageable very quickly. This can lead to metrics becoming the invisible monster behind the scenes. We have a number of customers that have 10 or more tools to monitor and measure the environment; many tools with duplicate functionality and most of which are not utilized to the fullest extent. Instead, they have several tools utilizing partial functionality to monitor limited aspects of the infrastructure and services. This can be one of the more wasteful facets of IT; think about this waste:

- Limited use of very expensive tools
- A host of servers to run the tools
- Storage to collect and manage the data
- Agents distributed across the infrastructure
- Network bandwidth utilization
- Personnel (installation, maintenance, training, etc.) to manage all of the above.

The costs of underutilized or wasted resources add up very quickly and yet this is not always considered during design. Metrics are often considered during the 'service transition' phase which can lead to impulse decisions such as quick tool purchases to fill perceived holes.

When developing metrics the proper theme should be 'early and often'.

- Begin developing metrics early in the design phase to ensure all aspects of the design are measureable and what metrics can be collected.
- Review the metrics often and make sure they will continue to provide value through transition. This will accommodate any changes in build or design found during transition. This will continue through the lifecycle and throughout the life of the service.

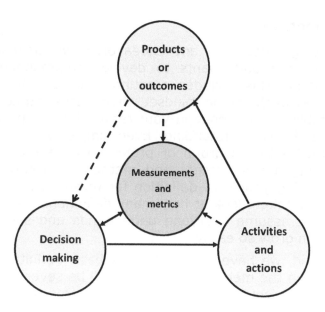

Figure 1 Metrics influence

Metrics can and should have an influence in the daily activities of the service provider. *Figure 1* demonstrates the sphere of influence metrics should have. Metrics are the centerpiece to ongoing successful delivery of services. Good decisions are made using experience gained from lessons learned and the measurements and metrics available. Those decisions form the measureable activities, and actions taken, to carry out the decision. Measurements from the activities and actions are collected and stored during execution. The activities and actions produce the measureable products or outcomes. The measurements and metrics are then used to:

- Improve the next set of decisions
- Improve the activities and actions increasing efficiency
- Ensure the products meet or exceed the requirements of the customers.

Defining metrics

Before moving forward on any endeavor, it will benefit all stakeholders and participants to develop commonality in communication. This includes creating a lexicon to help everyone stay in the same mindset when discussing certain topics. Establish consistency in your terminology to prevent confusion and misunderstanding. Even simple wording can cause turmoil within a group or project. This is the same when defining measurements and metrics. Therefore, we suggest creating your own definition for these basic terms. Go online and take a look at how many definitions there are for words we assume everyone understands and see how confusion can grow so easily.

With that said, we have provided a few basic definitions to start you down the metrics path. There will be several other terms that will require definition but the terms below are just to get things rolling.

- A measure is a quantifiable expression of performance collected during the execution of activities.

- A metric is a specific measurement or calculation associated with performance. Metrics are applied as references for assessing variance as compared to a defined target. Some metrics may reflect Key Performance Indicators (KPIs).

- A baseline is a known state or performance level that is used as a reference for subsequent measurements. It consists of a set of well characterized and understood measurements including all the phases of a process and the results. Baselines provide:
  - A comparison between the 'as is' and 'to be' states
  - Used for trending performance over time
  - Can help set a benchmark (achievement target)
  - Allows predictive modeling ('what if?' scenarios)
  - A fall back point for change.

Keep terminology and definitions simple and concise to ease the learning curve and to improve communication. As new terms do come up, take a few minutes to stop and gain consensus on the meaning and definition of these terms. Then document them and move on.

Why do we need metrics?

Good, quantifiable metrics provide a wealth of knowledge for support and management of processes and for the delivery of services to the customers. They help us to recognize the value of our processes and services and the benefits gained by the organization when using these services. Benefits of metrics include:

- Establishing baselines
- Presenting improvement opportunities
- Providing an understanding of current performance
- Eliminating assumptions
- Decreasing waste
- Managing costs.

This list can be extended once we find additional benefits in metrics. The bottom line is that metrics should be a constant staple for all decision making.

Reliable metrics give stakeholders confidence in the use and performance of their processes and services. Metrics provide an understanding of current issues, pain points, areas of concern, and areas of success.

Methodology for using metrics

To create consistency across the organization, we recommend developing a framework to generate and implement metrics. Whether it is called a 'process' or 'procedure' doesn't really matter, the priority is maintaining consistency in the creation of metrics. *Figure 2* illustrates a sample framework to help get started with a methodology that will fit your organization's requirements. Gather requirements from business owners and from the service

9

provider to understand all aspects of service provision. As part of the requirement, make sure AQLs are also collected. This will provide an understanding of the expectations which will eventually become the performance targets documented in the Service Level Agreement (SLA). Ensure all parties sign off on the requirements before continuing. The following points provide details for each step in the example framework found in *Figure 2*:

1. Based on the requirements, determine the metrics needed to provide performance information for the service, processes, outcomes, and the infrastructure. At this point, ensure the metric development activities are included in the Service Acceptance Criteria (SAC) which can be used as a quality checklist through the service lifecycle. These first two steps should occur early in your service lifecycle.

2. Once the metrics list is complete, distribute it to the business owners and members of the service provider to validate that the metrics will provide the necessary performance information. Take this through a formalized activity documenting:

   o All individuals who reviewed the metrics
   o All feedback
   o Actions items
   o Official approval (sign-off).

3. As part of design, review all appropriate tools to find if the capabilities to collect the metrics are available with the current toolset. There may be times when the current toolset does not have the functionality required to collect the measurements; if this occurs check if the vendor provides modules or upgrades that include your requirements. This will maintain the current toolset and manage the cost of an acquisition. This review should also consider if the current toolset does not provide the measurement

functions required, in this case a tool acquisition may be part of the overall design.

4. Have a third party, usually an engineer, review the metrics and selected tools to verify that the measurements and metrics meet the requirements of the stakeholders. An engineer will provide the technical skills required to ensure the tools can collect the agreed upon metrics. This too should be a formalized activity following similar steps to Activity 3. Once this final review is complete, ensure all requirements for the metrics are included in the Service Design Package (SDP).

5. Implement the metrics through the 'service transition' phase to build, test, and deploy the metrics into production (service operations). As the service or process is built, all aspects of metrics collection must be included in the release. This will ensure the metrics are put through the same rigor of testing as the other parts of the release. This is critical if the tool requires agents to be deployed to other servers or through firewalls (based on the information passing through). These transition activities will reduce possible issues that could arise in the operational environment.

These steps provide areas of consideration when creating your metrics activities. As you develop your methodology make sure you follow the service lifecycle phases treating this new process as any other production process or service.

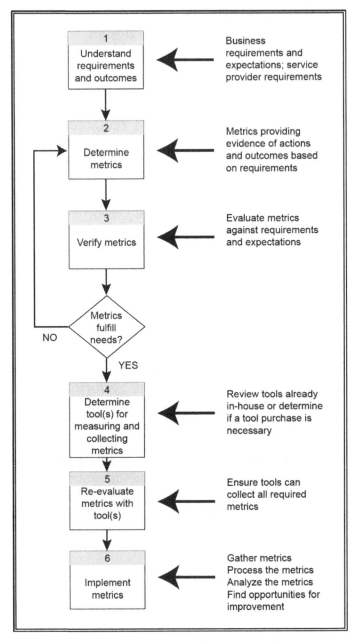

Figure 2 Metrics framework

You may notice that the approach defined in *Figure 2* closely follows the Seven-Step Improvement process (found in *ITIL*® *v3 Continual Service Improvement* (CSI)). This process provides a simple methodology for managing metrics and is a good starting point to create your own method. The organization's vision and mission statements can be used to offer guidance to the activities and help ensure the measurements and metrics continue to provide value. The following is a quick recap of the Seven-Step Improvement process[1]:

- Based on the business goals and objectives, services being delivered, and the methods used for delivery, define what should be measured. What should be measured are process activities and outcomes that are considered important for management decision making.

- Identify what actually can be measured with the tools employed, and performance data and information available in the knowledge base.

- Gather the metrics into defined repositories and check their integrity.

- Compile the metrics and apply them to the service delivery processes.

- Analyze the measurement results for validity (i.e. verify they measure what was intended to be measured), reliability (i.e. verify the measurements reflect actual performance characteristics) and accuracy (i.e. ensure there are no errors in the data or the calculations).

- Present the metrics results with summary conclusions indicated by the performance measurements.

- Implement corrective actions, including revised metrics as necessary to provide valuable decision support to the business.

---

[1] Cabinet Office (UK), *ITIL*®, *Continual Service Improvement* (London, England, The Stationery Office (TSO), 2011) 49-64

Purpose for metrics (metrics tree)

The variety of tools offered today provides extensive opportunities for collecting measurements. In fact, it is very easy to become overwhelmed with the amount of information available through these tools. Measurements and metrics require purpose; the organization must have a reason to collect and use measurements. This purpose can be found using the 'metrics tree' (*Figure 3*). The 'metrics tree' helps to establish measurement criteria and linkages to achieve success and provide purpose to your metrics. These criteria include:

- Focus on the vision and mission — ensure the vision and mission statements are consistently addressed throughout all levels of the 'metrics tree' as these provide the strategic direction of the organization.

- Maintain goals and objectives — maintain up-to-date goals and objectives as the organization continues to move forward and achieve successes. As goals and objectives are obtained, create new ones to keep the forward momentum.

- Develop Critical Success Factors (CSFs) — CSFs are required for an activity or project to accomplish the goals and objectives defined.

- Determine Key Performance Indicators (KPIs) —KPIs are quantifiable measurements in support of the CSFs.

- Select quantifiable measurements and metrics (customer requirements, outcomes, operational) — selective measurements and metrics provide the data and information needed to provide feedback and responses to the higher levels of the metrics tree.

- Identify intangible measurements — choose measurements and metrics that, while not monetary (tangible) by nature, provide insight into the softer aspects of a service or process. These can include stakeholder perception or comments, complaints, and compliments.

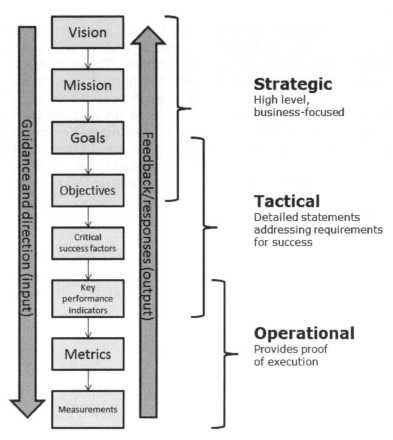

Figure 3 The metrics tree

Integrating metrics

By following the guidance above, you will begin to collect useful measurements and metrics from the tools that support your processes and services. While these individual measurements are important and have a purpose, in many cases a measurement doesn't offer full value by itself. Measurements and metrics should be integrated and combined to provide a complete picture of the situation at hand. Bringing these together creates context for these metrics which helps tell the story of success for our processes and services through the information gained from our efforts.

To fully understand all aspects of service provision, multiple metrics will provide both the purpose and meaning for the activities in support of our deliverables. These metrics will provide the evidence of the achievement of requirements and successful delivery of the expected outcomes. The combination of metrics will also help us understand whether a single metric is delivering good or bad news. For example, if metric 'A' shows a percentage increase in service desk calls, how do we know what it means? We need other metrics to support and bring clarity to metric 'A,' thus telling a story.

Metrics reporting

The value and benefits of metrics are delivered via a reporting structure. Reports provide the metrics information to stakeholders in multiple formats to address their needs and present the information in a usable manner. Of course, the basic requirements for reports must be understood and are derived from questions such as:

- Who is the audience?
- What information do they need?
- When do they need it?
- How do they get it?
- How will the report be used?
- What format do they prefer?

These questions must be asked for every report to ensure we are delivering the right information to the right audience. Developing a report questionnaire or standard report request will allow consistent information to be collected concerning the above questions. A good reporting structure will have a tremendous impact on customer satisfaction and communication.

For the most part, we use two basic mediums of report delivery: electronic or hard copy (paper). Today's preferred method is electronic as this provides greater flexibility in style, format, and usability. Electronic reports also offer an increased opportunity to measure report usage. These measurements include attributes such as:

- Number of hits per site
- Unique visitors
- Time spent on the report site
- Pages viewed per visit
- Most popular reports
- Most popular report pages.

The format of the report is also critical based on the diverse audience viewing the report. Again, electronic reporting can include basic reports, dashboards, drill-down reports, linked reports, etc., all of which increase the usage of reports by providing a more intuitive look and feel for the audience. This gives a more personal touch for each individual, allowing them to have basic customization features depending on the reporting tool.

Electronic reports also offer greater levels of information security and control. An issue we have seen is the number of individuals who have access to reporting tools to create ad hoc reports. While this is helpful to many people because of expediency, it also creates issues with security, standardization and communication (e.g., reports created and sent to anyone in and out of the organization). These uncontrolled reports (unknown number and audience) create an extremely large information and communication challenge. The organization can be sending mixed messages to their customers and stakeholders as one report may deliver 'good' news while another report on the same topic may deliver the opposite message. What message does that send, other than IT doesn't know what they are doing? We are quite sure that is not the message we want to deliver! To alleviate or prevent this issue, we recommend the following considerations:

- Standardize reporting (methodologies and formats)

- Create a reporting group or team
- Limit the number of reporting tools
- Limit access to reporting tools (gain control)
- Create a reporting service and put it in your service catalog.

These steps will provide high levels of consistency for all reports which will also create an auditable methodology for report management as well as improve aspects of knowledge management. Improvements in reporting communication and security will increase the perception of the service provider with the customers and stakeholders. And once again, this is a measureable approach.

Securing and protecting metrics

Metrics are vital to the organization's success and therefore, should be handled as highly valued knowledge assets. With that said, metrics provide information, via reports, that can create incredible amounts of knowledge which should be part of the Service Knowledge Management System (SKMS). Ultimately, as a service provider your metrics are part of your intellectual property.

As such, the repositories containing the measurements and metrics should be managed and tracked as Configuration Items (CIs); thus following the same processes and procedures used to manage the important components required to deliver services. This will ensure that these repositories are:

- Part of the SKMS
- Secured with limited write and update access
- Backed up regularly
- Stored on network storage devices
- Part of the contingency plan
- Audited regularly to ensure accuracy.

These steps will promote confidence in the data and information contained in the metrics repositories when making decisions or taking action.

Calculations

Many of the metric calculations found in this book are based on simplified formulas. While workable, these are not intended to be the 'end-all, be-all' calculations. As you mature your use of metrics, the formulas will evolve as additional measurements, new calculations, new/updated tools, or changes in technology all impact the methods used to calculate the metrics.

Metrics are normally calculated and presented in various forms such as numbers, ratios, percentages, and averages. These cover the majority of metric calculations in the industry and in this book. Flexibility is a key attribute to metrics with the ongoing changes in both business and technology that will require continued monitoring and review of the metrics for relevance. If you are using tools to collect measurements and calculate the metrics (the better solution in many cases), flexibility will be gained in the updates and upgrades provided by the suppliers. So, again, be creative and find ways to improve your measurements and metrics.

Continual Service Improvement (CSI)

All metrics have a role in CSI as they provide objective evidence of process or service improvement. Therefore, we do not have a CSI metrics chapter in this book. That, of course, doesn't mean that there are no CSI specific measurements or metrics. If you decide to develop CSI metrics, a good starting point would be to include CSI activities in all processes. As part of a process, a CSI activity will become inherent to the normal process flow providing regular opportunities to consistently review the process execution. This will create CSI measurements every time the process is executed.

CHAPTER 3: SERVICE STRATEGY METRICS

Service strategy provides guidance and direction for the provision and delivery of services through the service lifecycle. Strategy helps the organization to understand the outcomes and expectations of the business. Services are then delivered and supported by the processes found within the service lifecycle.

Strategy will begin with the vision and mission of the organization to create policies and plans for building a business focused culture and mindset throughout the department(s).

Strategy processes and metrics are used throughout the lifecycle ensuring that the processes and services continue to deliver business outcomes. The metrics in this chapter are tied to the processes found in *ITIL® Service Strategy*. Many of these metrics will continue to provide value through the remaining phases of the lifecycle. The metrics sections for this chapter are:

Strategy management metrics

Service portfolio management metrics

Financial management metrics

Demand management metrics

Business relationship management metrics.

Strategy management metrics

The metrics in this section support the Strategic Service Management (SSM) for IT process. These metrics are in line with several KPIs that support this process. The metrics presented in this section are:

- Number of services outsourced
- Number of market spaces defined
- Number of market spaces fulfilled
- Percentage of services with service valuation performed

- Percentage of IT staff with ITSM training
- Percentage of services with one customer
- Number of services monitored via dashboards.

Metric name

Number of services outsourced

Metric category

Strategy management

Suggested metric owner

Service manager

Typical stakeholders

Customers, management, financial manager, IT staff, suppliers, service level manager

Description

A sourcing strategy provides the opportunity to leverage the strengths of suppliers allowing them to fulfill gaps within the organization's environment. Benefits to outsourcing include:

- Leverage strengths of the supplier
  (i.e. knowledge and experience)
- Augmenting staff
- Potential financial savings
- Expedite service or process implementation
- Overcome entry barriers.

Justification for outsourcing must include multiple benefits for the entire organization. Focusing heavily on one benefit (i.e. cost savings) can and most likely will produce a negative future impact for the organization.

This metric will assist in understanding the number of services being fully or partially outsourced. It can help provide a good picture of where and how service assets are controlled.

Measurement description

Formula: N/A

This metric provides a high-level view of the outsourcing picture and should be used in conjunction with other metrics to provide a full understanding of the current levels of outsourcing as compared to the outsourcing strategy.

Frequency

> **Measured:** Quarterly
>
> **Reported:** Annually

Acceptable quality level: Create a baseline

> **Range:** Dependent on the needs of the customers and organization

Metric name

Number of market spaces defined

Metric category

Strategy management

Suggested metric owner

Service manager

Typical stakeholders

Customers, management, financial manager, service level manager

Description

Market spaces[2] are described as 'potential opportunities for exploitation by the IT organization'. These opportunities can lead to new or updated services which serve or facilitate the outcomes needed by the business. Opportunities can include:

- Growth in corporate sales
- Departmental changes
- Company expansion.

This metric provides insight to future services offered by IT. These defined market spaces demonstrates a more business focused IT department looking to serve customers now and into the future.

Measurement description

Formula: N/A

This metric should be monitored and tracked to ensure IT maintains a business focus and continuously searches for new market spaces to serve. This will also demonstrate a more proactive approach to managing the relationship with the business.

Frequency

> **Measured:** Quarterly
>
> **Reported:** Quarterly

Acceptable quality level: N/A

> **Range:** N/A

---

[2] Cabinet Office (UK), *ITIL®, Service Strategy* (London, England, The Stationery Office (TSO), 2011) 93

Metric name

Number of market spaces fulfilled

Metric category

Strategy management

Suggested metric owner

Service manager

Typical stakeholders

Customers, management, financial manager, service level manager

Description

This metric demonstrates the value provided by IT via those services that fulfill market spaces previously identified. Aligning with the business and understanding their needs will help IT provide services that address this need thus fulfilling the market space.

Market spaces are defined as opportunities, therefore an IT department that identifies and fulfills these is a proactive organization looking forward into the future.

Measurement description

Formula: N/A

Using this metric in combination with the 'market spaces defined' metric will demonstrate the value proposition of IT services as these market spaces fulfill true business need. This can also be used with 'service portfolio management' as services mature through the lifecycle.

Frequency

    Measured: Quarterly

    Reported: Annually

Acceptable quality level: N/A

    Range: N/A

Metric name

Percentage of services with service valuation performed

Metric category

Strategy management

Suggested metric owner

Service manager

Typical stakeholders

Customers, management, financial manager

Description

Service valuation can help determine the cost of delivering a service and the value of the service (benefit) to the business. Many organizations struggle with understanding the total cost of service delivery more from the value proposition than the cost factors. Determining costs is the easier of the two. However, value can be difficult to put into a financial perspective especially when dealing with intangibles. Financial expertise is required to help determine service valuation.

This metric will provide IT and the business with a better understanding of the financial implications of service provision as more services have a service valuation performed. Having financial knowledge of services increases the ability to make sound business decisions.

Measurement description

Formula:

$$\frac{\text{Services with service valuation}}{\text{Total number of services}} * 100$$

This metric will be gathered primarily within financial management; however, the knowledge gained from this will assist in decision making beginning at a strategic level. A service valuation can range from a group of simple financial calculations to a comprehensive financial assessment.

Frequency

  Measured: Quarterly

  Reported: Quarterly

Acceptable quality level: 90%

   Range: < 90% unacceptable

        = 90% acceptable

        > 90% exceeds

Metric name

Percentage of staff with ITSM training

Metric category

Strategy management

Suggested metric owner

Service manager

Typical stakeholders

Customers, management, financial manager, IT staff

Description

This metric demonstrates IT's commitment to service management, their staff and customers. Service management is a cultural change for the entire organization which requires all members of IT to establish a new business/customer focus. Quite frankly, this viewpoint is not natural for many IT people; their focus is more towards technology.

Formal training is one method to instill this new mindset throughout the organization. Therefore, tracking and reporting this metric is essential for IT to demonstrate to the business and customers the importance of service management and this new way of doing business.

Measurement description

Formula:

$$\frac{\text{Number of staff with ITSM training}}{\text{Total number of staff}} * 100$$

This metric might be looked at from two aspects. First, 'staff' can represent IT staff with ITSM training to understand the propagation of service management knowledge within IT. The second aspect might be from the customer view, demonstrating commitment to service management principles via customer training in ITSM.

Frequency

> **Measured:**   Quarterly

> **Reported:**   Annually

Acceptable quality level: 95%

> **Range:**   < 95% unacceptable

> = 95% acceptable

> > 95% exceeds

Metric name

Percentage of services with one customer

Metric category

Strategy management

Suggested metric owner

Service manager

Typical stakeholders

Customers, management, financial manager, IT staff, service level manager

Description

This metric provides an understanding of services dedicated to one customer. While some services will have only one customer, we should strive to create services that are shared by multiple customers. These shared services create higher levels of efficiency and can help reduce costs. However, there will still always be a need for those dedicated services required by a single customer.

Most organizations understand that a dedicated service could result in higher costs and an increase in unused resources. Reasons for a dedicated service might include:

- Security levels
- Financial information
- Privacy information
- Customer types.

Measurement description

Formula:

$$\frac{\text{Number of services with one customer}}{\text{Total number of services}} * 100$$

This metric should be continually monitored, regularly measured, and reported to the business at least annually. Financial management and capacity management metrics can be used in conjunction with this metric to show costs of dedicated services along with the utilization of components.

Frequency

Measured: Annually

Reported: Annually

Acceptable quality level: N/A

Range: N/A

Metric name

Number of services monitored via dashboards

Metric category

Strategy management

Suggested metric owner

Service manager

Typical stakeholders

Customers, management, financial manager, IT staff, service level manager

Description

Monitoring and reporting tools, such as dashboards, provide an easy method to display metric information for services, and the technology used to deliver the services. Dashboards are easy to use and understand as they provide real time information using simply graphics or charts. They provide value throughout the organization, including the customers.

This metric helps to understand the services being monitored and reported in a real time environment. This metric provides a sense of empowerment, as individuals can get the information they desire, but also in a format that is useful to them. This metric can also be used with other reporting media used by the organization.

Measurement description

Formula: N/A

The metric can be collected from one or multiple monitoring tools. The increased usage of dashboards demonstrates the organization's willingness to share and use information in an open and proactive manner.

While the focus of this metric is with dashboards, other types of monitoring and reporting tools (i.e. balanced scorecards) can be measured in the same manner.

Frequency

    Measured: Quarterly

    Reported: Quarterly

Acceptable quality level: N/A

    Range: N/A

Service portfolio management metrics

Service portfolio metrics provide insight to the life of a service. These metrics can be used in conjunction with service catalog metrics to improve support for the services. These metrics are in line with several KPIs that support this process. The metrics presented in this section are:

- Number of services in the service pipeline
- Percentage of services with documented customers
- Number of services in the approved state
- Percentage of services linked to business outcomes
- Percentage of services with documented risks.

Metric name

Number of services in the service pipeline

Metric category

Service portfolio management

Suggested metric owner

Product manager

Typical stakeholders

Customers, management, financial manager, IT staff, suppliers, service level manager

Description

The service pipeline is an important part of the service portfolio as it represents the future services offered by the service provider. Therefore, the pipeline should be monitored to ensure the provider continues to look forward to future service opportunities.

Services within the service pipeline are services that are in the theorizing, scoping, defining and analyzing stages of the service. These services will move from the pipeline to the service catalog when approved.

This metric will provide monitoring information that can be used for a current view of the pipeline as well as for historical trending of the pipeline. In either case, there is value in understanding the potential of future services in your inventory.

Measurement description

Formula: N/A

Depending on the tool utilized for the service portfolio, this metric can be collected using the functionality of the tool or it may require manual effort to extract the information.

Frequency

    Measured: Quarterly

    Reported: Annually

Acceptable quality level: Create a baseline and monitor

    Range: Dependent on opportunities found for future services

Metric name

Percentage of services with documented customers

Metric category

Service portfolio management

Suggested metric owner

Product manager

Typical stakeholders

Customers, management, financial manager, IT staff, suppliers, service level manager

Description

An important aspect of any service is the understanding of the customers who rely on that service. Many organizations have documentation focused on who their customers are but don't always understand what services the customers use or what value they receive from the services.

This metric provides insight to what services customers use. This increases the provider's understanding of the value of the service based on the customers. The value can be in both the quantity of customers and in the type customer such as:

- Executive
- External
- Financial
- Government.

Measurement description

Formula:

$$\frac{\text{Services with documented customers}}{\text{Total number of services}} * 100$$

This metric should be monitored and tracked to ensure IT maintains a count and knowledge of the customers, and the services they use. Integrating information from the service portfolio and a customer portfolio can help collect this metric. Dynamic organizations see constant fluctuations in customers which may require increased levels of monitoring.

Frequency

Measured: Quarterly

Reported: Quarterly

Acceptable quality level: N/A

Range: N/A

Metric name

Number of services in the approved state

Metric category

Service portfolio management

Suggested metric owner

Product manager

Typical stakeholders

Customers, management, financial manager, IT staff, suppliers, service level manager

Description

From a service portfolio viewpoint, approved services move from the service pipeline to the service catalog (both parts of the portfolio). Once approved, resources can be applied to create the service and ultimately implement the service into production for customer consumption.

This metric helps monitor those services that have been approved to move forward through the service lifecycle.

Measurement description

Formula: N/A

Using this metric in combination with other processes such as service catalog management and change management increases the awareness of service progression within the lifecycle. This can also increase the provider's control of services as they mature.

Frequency

> **Measured:** Quarterly
>
> **Reported:** Annually

Acceptable quality level: N/A

> **Range:** N/A

Metric name

Percentage of services linked to business outcomes

Metric category

Service portfolio management

Suggested metric owner

Product manager

Typical stakeholders

Customers, management, financial manager, IT staff, suppliers, service level manager

Description

IT services should help achieve the desired business outcomes for the customers. From a customer's viewpoint, value is achieved from the provision and support of services that produce deliverables that help obtain or achieve their outcomes. Value is derived from more than just the deliverables; increased efficiencies and cost control are aspects of a service that can help achieve these outcomes.

This metric will provide insight to those services that have demonstrated value to the customers in the form of achieving the outcomes of the business. While all services should provide value to the business, the services identified by this metric have proven that value proposition to the customers.

Measurement description

Formula:

$$\frac{\text{Services linked to business outcomes}}{\text{Total number of services}} * 100$$

This metric can be gathered from other processes such as business relationship management or service level management. Depending on the actual value provided, this metric can be collected from monitoring tools or from manual techniques such as meetings and surveys.

Frequency

    Measured: Quarterly

    Reported: Quarterly

Acceptable quality level: 90%

      Range: < 90% unacceptable

                  = 90% acceptable

                  > 90% exceeds

Metric name

Percentage of services with documented risks

Metric category

Service portfolio management

Suggested metric owner

Product manager

Typical stakeholders

Customers, management, financial manager, IT staff, suppliers, service level manager

Description

Risk is found in all phases and aspects of service provision. All action introduces some level of risk to the organization. This metric demonstrates the commitment of the provider to mitigate risk within service delivery. As risks are identified, they should be documented within a risk register or log which can provide input to this metric.

This metric provides an understanding of the amount of services provided that have a level of risk management applied. It does not account for the quality of risk management but simply a high level view of the extent of risk management within the organization.

Measurement description

Formula:

$$\frac{\text{Number of services with documented risks}}{\text{Total number of services}} * 100$$

Input for this metric can be provided from multiple resources such as risk management, security or auditing. No matter what the source, identified risks should be documented in a centralized repository to improve the quality of this metric.

Frequency

> **Measured:** Quarterly
>
> **Reported:** Quarterly

Acceptable quality level: N/A

> **Range:** N/A

Financial management metrics

Financial management provides critical information for enhanced decision making. Financial information may determine which new service is funded and which current services will continue to receive funding. Therefore, financial management provides value to the business and all stakeholders. These metrics are in line with several KPIs that support this process. Metrics within this section include:

- Percentage of financial reports delivered on time
- Percentage of services with ROIs achieved
- Percentage of budgets managed accurately (within acceptable ranges)
- Percentage of assets recorded with financial information.

Metric name

Percentage of financial reports delivered on time

Metric category

Financial management

Suggested metric owner

Finance manager, comptroller

Typical stakeholders

Customers, management, stakeholders

Description

Dependency on financial reports continues to grow as budget oversight and cost justification are scrutinized at all levels of the organization. Therefore, the 'on time' delivery of these reports is critical for management decision making.

This metric will assist in monitoring the distribution of financial reports to stakeholders. Report distribution times should be detailed in the SLA which provides a basis of comparison against the agreed upon timeframes.

Measurement description
Formula:

$$\frac{\text{Reports delivered on time}}{\text{Total reports delivered}} * 100$$

This metric should be monitored and collected regularly to ensure the ongoing distribution of financial reports. Report distribution can also have an impact on customer satisfaction.

Frequency
Measured: Monthly

Reported: Quarterly

Acceptable quality level: 95%
Range: < 95% unacceptable

= 95% acceptable

> 95% exceeds

Metric name
Percentage of services with ROIs achieved

Metric category
Financial management

Suggested metric owner
Finance manager, comptroller

Typical stakeholders
Customers, management, stakeholders

Description
We want to begin with the disclaimer: 'Be careful how you use this one'. There are issues associated with reporting ROI. There are multiple ways to define, calculate and use ROI thus potentially creating miscommunication. For our

purposes, ROI helps understand whether the organization is achieving a benefit (incrementally) for an investment made.

Determining ROI can be rather tricky as there are multiple ways to present your findings. This flexibility has both good and bad points which are beyond the scope of this book. Therefore, our focus will be on a simple ROI calculation which will demonstrate value by understanding financial payback. Simply put, value is gained as payback is received and fully achieved when the investment of the service is recouped.

This metric can assist in predicting the expected return in a business case or as gains toward the service investment.

Measurement description

Formula:

$$\frac{\text{Gains} - \text{investment costs}}{\text{Investment costs}} * 100$$

We recommend researching other ROI calculations and descriptions to improve your understanding if this description does not fit your needs. Also, consider using other metrics, such as risk management metrics, along with ROI to assist decision making.

Frequency

Measured: As required

Reported: As required

Acceptable quality level: Based on the business case presented

Range: Based on the timeline found in the business case

Metric name

Percentage of budgets managed accurately (within acceptable ranges)

Metric category

Financial management

Suggested metric owner

Finance manager, comptroller

Typical stakeholders

Customers, management, stakeholders

Description

Budget management is an integral part of a manager's monthly tasks. As mentioned earlier, budgets are scrutinized and, in many cases, are reviewed and reduced during the fiscal year. Actively monitoring budgets is essential to maintain accuracy of the monthly budget spend as well as the quarterly and annual roll-up.

This metric ensures that budgets are managed within the acceptable ranges (e.g. within three to five per cent) established by corporate finance.

Measurement description

Formula:

$$\frac{\text{Number of accurately managed budgets}}{\text{Total number of budgets}} * 100$$

This metric can be presented in a number of ways including:

- All monthly budgets within a division
- A roll-up of a departmental budget over a period of time
- A roll-up of all budgets annually

Frequency

> **Measured:** Monthly/quarterly

Reported: Quarterly/annually

Acceptable quality level: 98% budget accuracy

Range: < 98% unacceptable

= 98% acceptable

> 98% exceeds

Metric name

Percentage of assets recorded with financial information

Metric category

Financial management

Suggested metric owner

Finance manager, comptroller

Typical stakeholders

Customers, management, stakeholders

Description

The integration of processes is vital to the overall success of an ITSM program. Therefore, process metrics can be combined to provide a comprehensive view of process execution.

Financial information is collected and stored within each asset record based on the standard record content establish by asset management. This metric is measured by Service Asset and Configuration Management (SACM) but provides value to financial management.

Measurement description

Formula:

$$\frac{\text{Number of assets with financial information}}{\text{Total number of assets recorded}} * 100$$

The information for this metric can be managed by a configuration tool or asset management tool. Financial information can be provided by supplier tools, electronic documentation or manually entered.

Frequency

    Measured: Quarterly

    Reported: Annually

Acceptable quality level: 98%

    Range: < 98% unacceptable

                   = 98% acceptable

                   > 98% exceeds

Demand management metrics

Demand management helps us to understand how and when the customers work. Once fully understood, this information is used as input to proactive capacity management activities. The metrics presented in this section are:

- Percentage of services with PBAs
- Percentage of services with user profiles
- Number of capacity changes instigated by demand.

Metric name

Percentage of services with PBAs

Metric category

Demand management

Suggested metric owner

Demand manager

Typical stakeholders

Customers, management, capacity manager, business relationship manager, service level manager

Description

The metric provides a barometer of how well IT understands the business and how the business works. Patterns of Business Activity (PBAs) [3] provide input to capacity management helping adjust capacity to meet the changing needs of the business. PBAs allow IT to proactively manage capacity to better align IT with the business.

The dynamics of change in the IT world are well known as new technologies appear monthly. However, we must understand the business dynamics can have as many or

---

[3] Cabinet Office (UK), *ITIL®, Service Strategy* (London, England, The Stationery Office (TSO), 2011) 248-250

more changes due to the active nature of business. PBAs are a valuable tool for IT to help maintain that business focus and be more vigilant when it comes to business dynamics.

Measurement description

Formula:

$$\frac{\text{Number of services with PBAs}}{\text{Total number of services}} * 100$$

This metric should be monitored and collected regularly to ensure the PBAs are up to date and aligned with business activities.

Frequency

Measured: Quarterly

Reported: Annually

Acceptable quality level: 95%

Range: < 95% unacceptable

= 95% acceptable

> 95% exceeds

Metric name

Percentage of services with user profiles

Metric category

Demand management

Suggested metric owner

Demand manager

Typical stakeholders

Customers, management, capacity manager, business relationship manager, service level manager

Description

User Profiles (UPs)[4] provide an understanding of who is performing certain business activities and within the different PBAs. Combining PBA with UP gives IT complete knowledge of the business activity and who is performing the activity. UPs can include business groups such as:

- VIPs
- Staff from different offices
- Sales
- Project teams.
- Finance

This metric helps maintain a business focus as IT strives to provide the right service to the right people at the right time. Knowing who is performing an activity better equips IT to support those individuals and services in a more proactive manner.

Measurement description

Formula:

$$\frac{\text{Number of services with user profiles}}{\text{Total number of services}} * 100$$

We recommend using this metric with the 'services with PBAs' metric to provide a better view of how the business works and who performs the work. These are the types of metrics that allow IT to become more of a business partner throughout the organization.

Frequency

Measured: Quarterly

Reported: Annually

Acceptable quality level: 95%

Range: < 95% unacceptable

---

[4] Cabinet Office (UK), *ITIL®, Service Strategy* (London, England, The Stationery Office (TSO), 2011) 250-251

= 95% acceptable

> 95% exceeds

Metric name

Number of capacity changes instigated by demand

Metric category

Demand management

Suggested metric owner

Demand manager

Typical stakeholders

Customers, management, capacity manager, change manager, SACM

Description

This proactive metric is created from change management but allows IT to understand the impact of good demand management. Utilizing tools such as PBAs and UPs gives demand management the opportunity to instigate capacity changes prior to business need. This improves resource planning and demonstrates the increased value of IT to the business.

This metric should be presented to both IT and business management regularly as it shows the changing viewpoint of IT with proactive alignment to the dynamics of the business. This metric also demonstrates the benefit of process integration as demand, capacity, and change management work together in support of the business.

Measurement description

Formula: N/A

This type of metric provides insight to the relationships within IT and with the business. ITSM tools provide multiple ways to categorize and report changes. We suggest adjusting tool configurations and/or reports to provide this metric on a regular basis.

Frequency

    Measured: Monthly

    Reported: Quarterly

Acceptable quality level: N/A

    Range: Identify a potential baseline of changes and monitor for upward trends.

Business relationship management metrics

This process establishes relationships with the business and customers. Many of the activities and metrics from this process are closely aligned to service level management providing a more strategic viewpoint to services and the business. In some cases these two processes are combined due to limited resources or to simplify dealings with the business. However, we must ensure that the Business Relationship Manager (BRM) process activities remain at a strategic level. These metrics are in line with several KPIs that support this process. The metrics presented in this section are:

- Percentage of services with an assigned BRM
- Percentage of services with a business case
- Percentage of customers in the customer portfolio
- Number of complaints received (in a defined period)
- Average of customer satisfaction scores.

Metric name

Percentage of services with an assigned BRM

Metric category

Business relationship management

Suggested metric owner

Business relationship manager

Typical stakeholders

Customers, management, financial manager, IT staff, suppliers, service level manager

Description

Establishing a relationship with the business and customers is a critical aspect for a successful service management program. The business relationship manager will build and maintain this relationship, striving to understand the customer's needs and use that knowledge to develop business cases for new services. This role can be combined with the service level manager as responsibilities of both roles have many similarities.

This metric will help ensure that all services provided to the business have a BRM assigned. This will provide the customers consistency when dealing with the service provider.

Measurement description

Formula:

$$\frac{\text{Services with an assigned BRM}}{\text{Total number of services}} * 100$$

Data for this metric can be found within a service portfolio. How this data is extracted will depend upon the tool used to maintain the portfolio. We recommend creating regularly scheduled reports to ensure all services have an assigned BRM, and that the information is up to date.

Frequency

Measured: Quarterly

Reported: Annually

Acceptable quality level: 100% of business services

Range: All business services should have a BRM assigned

Metric name

Percentage of services with a business case

Metric category

Business relationship management

Suggested metric owner

Business relationship manager

Typical stakeholders

Customers, management, financial manager, IT staff, suppliers, service level manager

Description

The business case is a document that provides business information about a service and is used to justify funding for the service. This is not a technical document, it must be written from a business perspective in order to gain support from the authoritative body that approves the funding (e.g. finance board, executive committee).

This metric provides insight into the services that have gone through the proper funding and approval channels as the business case would be used as input to these steps. The business case provides valuable information concerning the business, and links the business needs to the service. The business case can be used as a:

- Funding and justification tool
- A planning document
- A educational document
- A requirements document (not for all service requirements).

Measurement description

Formula:

$$\frac{\text{Services with a documented business case}}{\text{Total number of services}} * 100$$

This metric can be collected from a document repository in conjunction with the service portfolio. It is possible that some legacy services may not have a business case. Depending on the service's age and status, a business case may not be necessary.

Frequency

>**Measured:** Quarterly
>
>**Reported:** Quarterly

Acceptable quality level: 90%

>**Range:** < 90% unacceptable
>
>= 90% acceptable
>
>> 90% exceeds

Metric name

Percentage of customers in the customer portfolio

Metric category

Business relationship management

Suggested metric owner

Business relationship manager

Typical stakeholders

Customers, management, financial manager, IT staff, suppliers, service level manager

Description

The customer portfolio contains all the information about the service provider's customers. This portfolio can be linked with other portfolios such as:

- Service portfolio
- Customer agreement portfolio
- Application portfolio
- Service catalog.

These links provide a holistic view of the services and the customers who use or depend on the services. Therefore, all portfolios should be maintained with up-to-date and accurate information.

This metric helps monitor the customers and ensures up-to-date information is maintained about each customer. This information will be used to support other processes throughout the service lifecycle.

Measurement description

Formula:

$$\frac{\text{Customers in the customer portfolio}}{\text{Total number of customers}} * 100$$

Many organizations may have difficulties understanding their total number of customers. If this is the case, then use this as a number to provide a count trending upward as more information about customers is collected.

Frequency

> **Measured:** Quarterly
>
> **Reported:** Annually

Acceptable quality level: 95%

> **Range:** < 95% unacceptable
>
> = 95% acceptable
>
> > 95% exceeds

Metric name

Number of complaints received (in a defined period)

Metric category

Business relationship management

Suggested metric owner

Business relationship manager

Typical stakeholders

Customers, management, IT staff, suppliers, service level manager

Description

Unfortunately, complaints are part of any service provider's daily or weekly dealings. While all service providers strive to provide the best possible service, there are times when they can't please everyone. The bottom line is, 'stuff happens' and we deal with it the best we can. Most individuals are good customers and, while they may not be happy with everything, they understand that failures and problems occur. However, they do expect their service restored as quickly as possible.

This metric will provide insight to the number of issues that occur with customers. Customer complaints must be taken seriously and handled personally. Do not use automated tools to respond to complaints. This is a major part of the BRM role. Allow them to handle complaints personally and professionally which will help build a stronger relationship with that customer.

Measurement description

Formula: N/A

This metric can be gathered from the service catalog, service desk or from the BRM. Complaints should be collected and counted within a specific timeframe such as monthly or quarterly. This number can serve as a baseline and trended, hopefully downward, over like periods in the future.

Just remember, it is equally important to collect and measure compliments received. We recommend developing a similar metric for compliments.

Frequency

Measured: Quarterly

Reported: Quarterly

Acceptable quality level: N/A
> **Range:**   N/A

Metric name

Average of customer satisfaction scores

Metric category

Business relationship management

Suggested metric owner

Business relationship manager

Typical stakeholders

Customers, management, financial manager, IT staff, suppliers, service level manager

Description

There are a number of methods to collect customer satisfaction levels or scores. This metric demonstrates the current level of customer satisfaction. Most organizations plan some type of customer satisfaction survey during the year. These surveys are used as a barometer to measure satisfaction levels over a variety of topics including:

- The service (availability, performance, etc.)
- Support
- Staff professionalism
- Fulfillment (are they getting what they need?).

This metric provides an understanding of how the customers feel about the services they are receiving from the service provider during a defined period of time. These types of surveys measure the organization as a whole while other surveys, such as from the service desk, measure the immediate service received. These surveys provide value throughout the year and help the service provider make ongoing adjustments to improve the service.

Measurement description

Formula:

There are several methods used to calculate surveys that can become quite elaborate based on the type and size of the survey. We recommend using a known survey tool to help create the survey and to provide built-in calculations and reports to expedite processing of survey results.

Survey tools provide an easy method to collect and report survey information in a variety of ways. These tools also provide greater levels of consistency and dependability of the information collected.

Frequency

> **Measured:** Semi-annually / annually
>
> **Reported:** Annually

Acceptable quality level: 90% satisfied (a baseline to improve)

> **Range:** < 90% unacceptable
>
> = 90% acceptable
>
> > 90% exceeds

CHAPTER 4: SERVICE DESIGN METRICS

Metrics for service design processes provide the capability to evaluate designs of new or changed services for transition into an operational state. These metrics are used to objectively assess the effectiveness of new or changed service designs to deliver the intended service capabilities. The metrics sections for this chapter are:

Design co-ordination metrics

Service catalog metrics

Service level management metrics

Availability management metrics

Capacity management metrics

IT service continuity management metrics

Information security management metrics

Supplier management metrics.

Design co-ordination metrics

Service design activities must be properly co-ordinated to ensure the service design goals and objectives are met. The Design co-ordination process encompasses all activities for the centralized planning, co-ordination and control of service design activities and resources across design projects and the service design phase of the service lifecycle.

The extensiveness of design co-ordination efforts will vary depending on the complexity of the new or changed service designs. Formalized process structure prescribed by the organization (i.e. governance) also impacts the level of effort necessary to perform service design co-ordination activities. The metrics presented in this section are:

- Number of Service Design Packages (SDP) rejected
- Number of designs rejected
- Percentage of designs associated with projects
- Number of architectural exceptions

- Percentage of designs without approved requirements
- Percentage of designs with reusable assets
- Percentage of staff with skills to management designs.

Metric name

Number of Service Design Packages (SDPs) rejected

Metric category

Design co-ordination

Suggested metric owner

Engineering or service management

Typical stakeholders

Technical staff, engineering, service transition, applications

Description

An SDP is a collection of documents created throughout the service design phase of the service management lifecycle. It contains all the documentation necessary for the transition (build, test, deploy) of the service or process into the production environment including:

- Requirements (customer, technical, operational)
- Design diagrams
- Financial documentation (business case, budgets)
- Testing documentation
- Service acceptance criteria
- Plans (transition, operational).

Therefore, the transition team must have the authority to reject an SDP and provide justification for the rejection.

This metric will assist in tracking the rejected SDPs to provide valuable information for improvements within the service design phase. Over time this metric can help improve future designs and improve the services and processes that are used in the production environment.

Measurement description

Formula: N/A

This metric, a simple tally (count) used for comparison over time, should be monitored and collected regularly to ensure progress is made in designing services and processes. This will also demonstrate a more proactive approach to managing the environment.

Frequency

> **Measured:** Monthly
>
> **Reported:** Quarterly

Acceptable quality level: Create a quarterly baseline and reduce the number of SDPs rejected over time

> **Range:** Dependent on the established baseline

Metric name

Number of designs rejected

Metric category

Design co-ordination

Suggested metric owner

Engineering management

Typical stakeholders

Technical staff, engineering, service transition, applications, architecture

Description

Designs are created in the service design phase of the service management lifecycle. These designs are based on requirements and organizational standards to ensure supportable services and processes are found in production. A design can be rejected based on documented reasons such as:

- Missing customer requirements
- Missing operational requirements
- Not following architectural standards
- Improper or mission documentation.

This metric provides insight into the service design phase. As designs are created, they are reviewed to ensure compliance to criteria such as:

- Policies
- Architectures

- Business needs
- Regulatory requirements.

This metric can assist in improving the level of collaboration and communication with the various design teams.

Measurement description

Formula: N/A

This metric should be monitored and tracked (by both project management and service management) regularly to ensure all aspects and criteria of the design fulfill the requirements of the customer and the business. This will also demonstrate a more proactive approach to managing the environment.

Frequency

Measured: Monthly

Reported: Quarterly

Acceptable quality level: Create a quarterly baseline and reduce the number of designs rejected over time

Range: Dependent on the established baseline

Metric name

Percentage of designs associated with projects

Metric category

Design co-ordination

Suggested metric owner

Engineering or project management

Typical stakeholders

Project management office, engineering, change management

Description

This metric demonstrates the link between designs and project management. Utilizing project management throughout the lifecycle greatly increases the opportunity for success as project managers provide management skills that are typically not inherent within many IT organizations.

As the number of designs associated with projects increases, planning the staffing and resources required for the service or process will improve both the timeline and financial considerations.

Measurement description

Formula:

$$\frac{\text{Designs associated with projects}}{\text{Total number of designs}} * 100$$

Using this metric in combination with the rejected SDPs and rejected design metrics will possibly demonstrate the benefits found in using project management. This can also be used with change management metrics to ensure change compliance and process integration.

Frequency

    Measured: Monthly

    Reported: Quarterly

Acceptable quality level: Create a quarterly baseline

    Range: Create the acceptable quality range from the baseline

Metric name

Number of architectural exceptions

Metric category

Design co-ordination

Suggested metric owner

Engineering or architectural management

Typical stakeholders

Engineering, architecture, management

Description

Architectural standards create consistency throughout the entire organization. These standards improve not only the designs but also:

- Testing
- Deployment
- Maintenance
- Service delivery
- Financial management.

Therefore, exceptions to any architectural standard should be monitored and managed to the lowest possible number. This metric increases awareness to the exceptions and should be directly reported to management to ensure full approval/authorization of the exception.

Measurement description

Formula: N/A

Combined with other metrics from change, incident and problem management will provide a clear indication of potential issues with exceptions including:

- Lack of staff knowledge
- Increased costs
- Changes to maintenance routines
- Testing
- Operational processes and procedures.

Frequency

Measured: Monthly

Reported: Monthly

Acceptable quality level: < 1%

Range: > 1% unacceptable

< 1% acceptable

0% exceeds

Metric name

Percentage of designs without approved requirements

Metric category

Design co-ordination

Suggested metric owner

Engineering management

Typical stakeholders

Customers, engineering, management

Description

This metric can be used by management and the design team to ensure the appropriate requirements have been collected and approved prior to moving forward with the design. Requirements drive the design of services and processes, and must be agreed upon by the relevant parties to understand what is to be delivered.

There are several different requirements types for any design. These requirements are collected at multiple stages within the design phase due to dependencies. Requirement types can include:

- Business
- Customer
- User

- Regulatory
- Operational
- Technical.

Whatever requirements are necessary to good design should be included within the project plan to ensure proper approval.

Measurement description

Formula:

$$\frac{\text{Designs without approved requirements}}{\text{Total number of designs}} * 100$$

Collection of data for this metric may be a manual effort depending on tool availability. This metric can be tracked within a project management tool or a repository for designs.

Frequency

> **Measured:** Monthly
>
> **Reported:** Quarterly

Acceptable quality level: < one per cent

> **Range:** > 1% unacceptable
>
> < 1% acceptable
>
> 0% exceeds (this should ultimately be the AQL)

Metric name

Percentage of designs with reusable assets

Metric category

Design co-ordination

Suggested metric owner

Engineering management or asset management

Typical stakeholders

Technical staff, engineering, management

Description

This metric provides an understanding of the level of efficiency for asset utilization. Reusable assets enhance the design effort by offering a known commodity to the design which will:

- Decrease design time
- Reduce costs
- Reduce test time
- Increase consistency.

Reusable assets may include:

- Hardware and software modules
- Documents
- Data elements
- Designs.

This metric will provide management with an indication of maturity for the design phase. As the number of reusable assets increases, other metrics (i.e. incident management, problem management) should see a gradual improvement.

Measurement description

Formula:

$$\frac{\text{Number of designs with reusable assets}}{\text{Total number of designs}} * 100$$

This metric should be continually monitored and reported to stakeholders. Integration with other metrics will help demonstrate the cause and effect of reusable assets within other processes.

Frequency

> **Measured:** Monthly
>
> **Reported:** Quarterly

Acceptable quality level: Create a quarterly baseline and increase designs with reusable assets over time

> **Range:** Dependent on the established baseline

Metric name

Percentage of staff with skills to management designs

Metric category

Design co-ordination

Suggested metric owner

Engineering management

Typical stakeholders

Technical staff, engineering, management

Description

This metric can be gathered from a human resources department, training records or a skills inventory/matrix. The metric provides an understanding of the skills available, within the organization, to build and manage aspects of a design.

This metric is vital when considering technologies or planning for training (i.e. budget, time, resources). This metric can be used to enhance decision making prior to the launch of the design and could impact the attributes of the design components.

Measurement description

Formula:

$$\frac{\text{Number of staff with required skills}}{\text{Total number of staff}} * 100$$

A skills matrix may be the best tool to understand and measure the skills required to deploy a service or process into production.

Frequency

> **Measured:** Quarterly
>
> **Reported:** Quarterly

Acceptable quality level: Primary and backup skills required

> **Range:** N/A

Service catalog management metrics

A service catalog presents the details of all services offered to those with approved access. It contains specific details (e.g. dependencies, interfaces, constraints, etc.) in accordance with the established service catalog management policies. The process objectives are to manage the service catalog with current and accurate information, ensure it is available to those with approved access, and ensure it supports the ongoing needs of other processes.

The scope of service catalog management encompasses maintaining accurate information for all services in the operational stage and services being prepared to go to an operational state. Timely catalog updates to reflect newly released services/service packages should be part of the overall service change. Applied service catalog management metrics should be based on the established process goals and specific Key Performance Indicators (KPIs). The service catalog management metrics presented in this section are:

- Percentage of services in the service catalog
- Percentage of customer facing services
- Percentage of service catalog variance
- Number of changes to the service catalog
- Percentage of service requests made via the service catalog
- Percentage increase in service catalog utilization
- Percentage of support services linked to CIs.

Metric name

Percentage of services in the service catalog

Metric category

Service catalog management

Suggested metric owner

Service catalog manager

Typical stakeholders

Customers, IT staff, management

Description

This metric provides an understanding of the amount of services that are documented in the service catalog. The metric can be used periodically throughout the life of the service catalog to ensure all services have a catalog entry.

However, during the transition/migration to the service catalog is when this metric can provide great value. This metric can assist in tracking the progress of moving services into the catalog.

This metric will become increasingly important as customers begin to use the service catalog more often.

Measurement description

Formula:

$$\frac{\text{Number of services in the catalog}}{\text{Total number of services}} * 100$$

This metric should be monitored and collected regularly to ensure all services are entered into the service catalog.

Frequency

> **Measured:** Monthly

> **Reported:** Quarterly

Acceptable quality level: 98%

> **Range:** < 98% unacceptable

> = 98% acceptable

> 100% exceed

Metric name

Percentage of customer-facing services

Metric category

Service catalog management

Suggested metric owner

Service catalog manager

Typical stakeholders

Customers, IT staff, management

Description

While similar to the previous metric, this metric deals with measuring services found in the service catalog. The difference however, is that this metric focuses on those services that can be used by the customer.

This metric will have a direct correlation with the usage of the catalog from the user base. If the service catalog is actionable (allow users to make service requests from the catalog) users will come to rely on the catalog to perform and/or make the majority of their requests to IT.

Therefore, IT must strive to have all customer-facing services populated within the service catalog. This will also give the users as sense of empowerment as they can manage and monitor their own requests.

Measurement description

Formula:

$$\frac{\text{Number of customer-facing services}}{\text{Total number of services}} * 100$$

These metrics should be monitored and tracked regularly to ensure an increased service catalog utilization to fulfill the service requests made from the customers.

Frequency

    Measured: Monthly

    Reported: Quarterly

Acceptable quality level: Establish the baseline and trend over time.

    Range: N/A

Metric name

Percentage of service catalog variance

Metric category

Service catalog management

Suggested metric owner

Service catalog manager

Typical stakeholders

Customers, IT staff, management

Description

This metric will assist in monitoring the accuracy of the service catalog entries. Regular reviews or audits of the catalog must be conducted to ensure the information in the catalog entry matches the functionality and attributes of the actual service. The review can include catalog features such as:

- Service attributes
- Service description
- Pricing
- Grammar and spelling
- Service availability.

The accuracy of the service catalog is paramount to the success of the services offered and the catalog. Customers must feel confident in the information provided within the service catalog in order to make and/or continue making the appropriate service request.

Measurement description

Formula: This formula provides a high level view of service in error.

$$\frac{\text{Reviewed services found in error}}{\text{Total number of services reviewed}} * 100$$

$$\frac{\text{Reviewed attributes found in error}}{\text{Total number of attributes reviewed}} * 100$$

The second formula provides a granular view into the services. Using these formulas together gives a better perspective of the catalog accuracy.

Frequency

Measured: Monthly

Reported: Quarterly

Acceptable quality level: Create a quarterly baseline

Range: 100% accuracy

Metric name

Number of changes to the service catalog

Metric category

Service catalog management

Suggested metric owner

Service catalog manager or change manager

Typical stakeholders

Customers, IT staff, management

Description

Changes to the service catalog are inevitable but change also increases the potential of errors in the catalog.

Therefore, this metric provides insight to changes that impact the service catalog and service offerings.

Monitoring and tracking change can assist in making decisions to review or audit the service catalog. If a high volume of changes occur within a period of time a catalog review might be warranted to ensure catalog accuracy.

This metric can also help to align service changes to catalog changes to again ensure catalog accuracy.

Measurement description

Formula: N/A

Regular tracking of this metric will provide a greater understanding of service change and the impact to the service catalog. The tracking can also trigger a review based on a pre-defined number of changes within a defined time period. Combining this metric with the previous metric will provide an increased level of assurance for the service catalog.

Frequency

> **Measured:**   Monthly
>
> **Reported:**   Monthly

Acceptable quality level: N/A

> **Range:**   N/A

Metric name

Percentage of service requests made via the service catalog

Metric category

Service catalog management

Suggested metric owner

Service catalog manager or service desk manager

Typical stakeholder

Customers, service owners, management

Description

An actionable service catalog provides increased benefits for all stakeholders. These benefits may include:

- Improved information of service offerings
- Better turnaround time for requests
- Decreased IT staff workload
- Customer empowerment
- Increased customer satisfaction.

This upward trending metric will demonstrate not only the utilization of the service catalog but also the potential increase in customer satisfaction. As customers become familiar with the catalog and how to use it, their satisfaction level may increase due to the enhanced functionality of the catalog and availability to service requests.

Measurement description

Formula:

$$\frac{\text{Requests made through the catalog}}{\text{Total number of service requests}} * 100$$

Collection of data for this metric may be a manual effort depending on tool availability. This metric can be tracked within a project management tool or a repository for designs.

Frequency

> **Measured:** Monthly
>
> **Reported:** Quarterly

Acceptable quality level: <5%

> **Range:** > 5% unacceptable
>
> < 5% acceptable

> 0% exceeds (this should ultimately be the AQL)

Metric name

Percentage increase in service catalog utilization

Metric category

Service catalog management

Suggested metric owner

Service catalog manager

Typical stakeholders

Customers, IT staff, management

Description

This metric provides an understanding of the acceptance of the service catalog as a single point of entry to seeing the services available and requesting those services. As services are added to the service catalog, customers should increase their utilization of the catalog to increase their productivity. Catalog offerings can include:

* Requesting services
* Referencing service information
* Asking questions
* Requesting changes
* FAQs.

A good service catalog empowers customers and frees the IT staff to perform other value added activities. To increase utilization, understand the customer's needs and provide for those through an intuitive, easy to use catalog.

Measurement description

Formula:

$$\frac{\text{Number of accesses to the catalog}}{\text{Previous number of accesses}} - 1 * 100$$

This metric should be over a standard period of time (i.e. weekly, monthly) for accurate utilization of the results. The metric will provide a new baseline during the reporting period and used for trending.

Frequency

> **Measured:** Monthly

> **Reported:** Quarterly

Acceptable quality level: Create a baseline and compare regularly

> **Range:** Dependent on the established baseline

Metric name

Percentage of support services linked to CIs

Metric category

Service catalog management

Suggested metric owner

Service catalog manager or configuration manager

Typical stakeholders

IT staff, configuration management, change management, release management

Description

Support services may not have direct value to the business but they do provide value in support of business services and processes. The metric will provide an understanding of the Configuration Items (CIs) linked to the support service. Having this understanding during the design phase allows greater levels of insight into the service when making design changes or integrating with other services.

Having increased knowledge of the CIs linked to a service during design ensures the correct resources and skills are available to enhance the overall design and service. This metric can be used to enhance decision making when considering the architecture and attributes of the service.

Measurement description
Formula:

$$\frac{\text{Number of support service linked to CIs}}{\text{Total number of support services}} * 100$$

Integration with the Configuration Management System (CMS) is required for the accuracy of this metric. This will provide a holistic view of the support service and the infrastructure used to provide the service.

Frequency

Measured: Monthly

Reported: Quarterly

Acceptable quality level: N/A

Range: N/A

Service level management metrics

Service level management is a vital service design process. It has the responsibility for identifying and documenting Service Level Requirements (SLRs) and establishing formal Service Level Agreements (SLAs) for every IT service offered.

Service level targets must accurately reflect customer expectations and user needs. Likewise, the service provider must be able to deliver services that meet or exceed targets in the established SLAs. The service level management process ensures that implemented (i.e. operational) and planned IT services are delivered in accordance with achievable performance targets. Service Level Management (SLM) efforts entail defining and documenting service level targets; monitoring, objectively measuring delivered service levels based on SLAs; reporting to customers and business management on actual service level performance; and participating in service improvement actions. The metrics presented in this section are:

- Percentage of SLA targets threatened
- Percentage of SLA targets breached
- Percentage of services with SLAs
- Number of service review meetings conducted
- Percentage of OLAs reviewed annually
- Number of CSI initiatives instigated by SLM
- Percentage of service reports delivered on time.

Metric name

Percentage of SLA targets threatened

Metric category

Service level management

Suggested metric owner

Service level manager

Typical stakeholders

Customers, IT staff, management

Description

Service level targets are found in the agreed upon SLAs established between the customer and service provider. Measurements taken against these targets and thresholds are set for monitoring to ensure proper delivery of the service. This metric is based on the target thresholds set within a monitoring tool.

This is a proactive metric which demonstrates the amount of alerts received within a defined period of time. Benefits of this metric include:

- Number of alerts based on the number of targets monitored
- Discovering potential problems before they occur
- The prevention of service outages
- The proactive efforts of the provider
- The quality of service monitoring.

Measurement description

Formula:

$$\frac{\text{Number of targets with alerts}}{\text{Total number of targets monitored}} * 100$$

This metric should be monitored and collected regularly to ensure all monitored targets are within their normal capacity, availability, and performance ranges.

Frequency

> **Measured:** Weekly
>
> **Reported:** Monthly

Acceptable quality level: Establish a baseline and trend over time

Range: Set the quality range from the baseline

Metric name

Percentage of SLA targets breached

Metric category

Service level management

Suggested metric owner

Service level manager

Typical stakeholders

Customers, IT staff, management

Description

While similar to the previous metric, this metric focuses on SLA targets that have been breached or failed. This metric should reflect a downward trend and will impact on the overall service quality delivered. Breached targets can:

- Increase potential downtime
- Impact business performance
- Create a reactive environment
- Damage the reputation of the organization
- Harm the relationship with the customer.

IT must understand the importance of the SLA targets and closely monitor these targets to ensure service delivery. Target breaches can be caused by:

- Poor understanding of service requirements
- Improper thresholds
- Spikes in demand
- Component failure.

Measurement description

Formula:

$$\frac{\text{Number of targets breached}}{\text{Total number of targets monitored}} * 100$$

These metrics can be represented with a percentage. However, some organizations may find more value in using an actual count. In either case, this metric must be reported to customers and management.

Frequency

>**Measured:** Weekly
>
>**Reported:** Monthly

Acceptable quality level: 1%

>**Range:** > 1% unacceptable
>
>= 1% acceptable
>
>< 1% exceeds

Metric name

Percentage of services with SLAs

Metric category

Service level management

Suggested metric owner

Service level manager

Typical stakeholders

Customers, IT staff, management

Description

This metric will assist in monitoring the progress of service level management as more services are documented with agreed upon SLAs. A well-documented SLA will help improve:

- Service delivery
- Customer relationships
- Process performance
- Business services
- Organizational performance.

SLAs are based on business requirements and expectations. These will help IT better understand the business and how the business operates, thus transforming IT from a technology provider to a service provider. Everyone wins.

Measurement description

Formula:

$$\frac{\text{Total services with SLAs}}{\text{Total number of services}} * 100$$

The metric is a catalyst facilitating the use of SLM metrics as well as other process metrics. Monitor this metric closely and regularly report SLM progress to all stakeholders.

Frequency

> **Measured:** Monthly/quarterly

> **Reported:** Quarterly/annually

Acceptable quality level: 100%

> **Range:** Set achievement goals over time

Metric name

Number of service review meetings conducted

Metric category

Service level management

Suggested metric owner

Service level manager

Typical stakeholders

Customers, IT staff, management

Description

Service review meetings must be documented in the SLA. This binds the customer and the service provider into an ongoing partnership to manage the service.

Based on the level of importance of the service, review meetings can be conducted monthly, quarterly or annually. Meeting documents such as agendas, attendance sheets, and meeting notes provide evidence of the meetings and of this metric.

This metric demonstrates the ongoing pursuit of service excellence as SLM continuously works with the business and IT to deliver services that fulfill the business's requirements.

Measurement description

Formula: N/A

Regular tracking of this metric can show how IT is attempting to better serve the business. Meeting schedules will provide input for the metric while meeting artifacts provide evidence.

Frequency

> **Measured:** Monthly
>
> **Reported:** Monthly

Acceptable quality level: N/A

> **Range:** N/A

Metric name

Percentage of OLAs reviewed annually

Metric category

Service level management

Suggested metric owner

Service level manager

Typical stakeholders

Customers, service owners, management

Description

As OLAs help define the levels of support required to deliver a service, it is vital that they are regularly reviewed to ensure they are up to date and relevant to meet the needs of the service. All parties associated with the OLA must participate in the OLA review to make certain all aspects of support are properly maintained and can continue to meet or exceed the targets established within the OLA.

This metric should reflect an upward trend and will demonstrate SLM's continued commitment to the delivery and ongoing support of the service. As support groups become familiar with the SLM process and the OLAs their understanding of the service and all aspects of the service will increase. This new found understanding and knowledge will help build the relationships within the IT organization and with the customer.

Measurement description

Formula:

$$\frac{\text{Number of OLAs reviewed annually}}{\text{Total number of OLAs}} * 100$$

Collection of data for this metric may be a manual effort depending on how OLAs are created, tracked and stored.

Frequency

> **Measured:** Monthly
>
> **Reported:** Quarterly

Acceptable quality level: 98%

> **Range:**   < 98% unacceptable
>
> = 98% acceptable
>
> > 99% exceed

Metric name

Number of CSI initiatives instigated by SLM

Metric category

Service level management

Suggested metric owner

Service level manager

Typical stakeholders

Customers, IT staff, management

Description

This metric is a simple tally (count) that provides an understanding of the service improvement initiatives started by SLM. The proactive nature of SLM should be a natural feed to service improvements as the service level manager:

- Monitors service performance
- Compares performance against SLA targets
- Meets with customers regularly
- Monitors OLAs
- Works with other ITSM processes and IT groups.

The efforts of SLM can discover opportunities for improvement and start the improvement process as early as possible. In many cases, this can occur much sooner than normal lines of communication.

Measurement description

Formula: N/A

This metric will demonstrate the proactive nature of SLM and increase the relationship with all SLM stakeholders including:

- Customers
- Service owners
- Management
- CSI manager
- Other process managers.

Frequency

> **Measured:** Monthly
> **Reported:** Quarterly

Acceptable quality level: N/A

> **Range:** N/A

Metric name

Percentage of service reports delivered on time

Metric category

Service level management

Suggested metric owner

Service level manager

Typical stakeholders

Customers, service owner, management

Description

As organizations move toward a more service-oriented environment, service reporting is becoming a critical component for managing services. Management depends on reports to review service delivery and improve decision making. Therefore, on-time delivery of these reports must be monitored to ensure stakeholders are up to date with regards to service performance and delivery.

This metric can help ensure service reports are created and delivered as required to the appropriate stakeholders. Reporting requirements should be contained within the SLA and measured using this metric.

Measurement description
Formula:

$$\frac{\text{Number of service reports delivered on time}}{\text{Total number of service reports delivered}} * 100$$

Regular monitoring of this metric will help the organization maintain consistency in report delivery and help increase customer satisfaction as on-time delivery meets or exceeds customer expectations.

Frequency
Measured: Monthly

Reported: Quarterly

Acceptable quality level: 98%
Range: < 98% unacceptable

= 98% acceptable

> 99% exceed

Availability management metrics

The availability management process is central to the IT service value proposition. Service utility (i.e. fitness for purpose and fitness for use)[5] cannot be realized without sustained delivery of services that meet the prescribed availability levels. Service availability is initially considered as part of setting objectives in service strategy generation, validated for realism/achievability and incorporated as part of service design, verified through testing in the operating environment as part of service transition, and continuously monitored in service operation.

Availability management process activities are intended to ensure that the reliability of delivered IT services meet availability targets defined in SLAs and is concerned with both current and planned service availability needs. The availability management process metrics presented in this section are:

- Service availability percentage
- Percentage of services with availability plans
- Percentage of incidents caused by unavailability
- Percentage of availability threshold alerts
- Percentage of services that have been tested for availability
- Mean Time Between Failures (MTBF)
- Mean Time Between Service Incidents (MTBSI)
- Mean Time To Restore Service (MTRS)
- Mean Time To Repair (MTTR)
- Percentage of services classified as vital business functions.

---

[5] Cabinet Office (UK), *ITIL®, Service Strategy* (London, England, The Stationery Office (TSO), 2011) 17-18

Metric name

Service availability percentage

Metric category

Availability management

Suggested metric owner

Service level manager

Typical stakeholders

IT operations manager, service manager, customer relationship manager, customers

Description

This is a measurement of the availability of a discrete service asset expressed as a percentage of the total time the service functionality is operationally available to the user. The metric applies MTBSI, MTTR and MTRS values from incident management records.

- MTBSI is calculated by subtracting the recorded date/time of a previous incident from the subsequently recorded incident for the specific service asset.

- MTRS represents the average time between implementing action(s) to correct/repair the root cause of a failure to the time when the service functionality is restored to the user. It includes service restoration testing and user acceptance times.

- MTTR is the sum of the detection time + response time + repair time.

Measurement description

Formula:

$$\frac{MTBSI-(MTTR+MTRS)}{MTBSI} * 100$$

Frequency

> **Measured:** Monthly
>
> **Reported:** Monthly

Acceptable quality level: 99.9%

> **Range:** < 99.9% unacceptable (service levels possibly out of control)
>
> = 99.9% acceptable (maintain/improve)
>
> > 99.9% exceeds (indicates well-managed service delivery)

Note

An AQL should be established for the specific service asset (system, subsystem, application, etc.). In a 24/7 operating environment, the AQL of 99.9% allows unavailability (downtime) of 8.76 hours/year or 43.8 minutes/month or 10.11 minutes/week.

Metric name

Percentage of services with availability plans

Metric category

Availability management

Suggested metric owner

Service level manager

Typical stakeholders

IT operations manager, service manager, customer relationship manager, customers

Description

This metric demonstrates the successful implementation of the availability management process as part of service delivery best practices. It shows the percentage of services with availability plans to document methods and techniques for achieving availability targets defined in SLAs.

The measurement is useful as an indicator of the validity of service design practices.

Measurement description
Formula:

$$\frac{\text{Number of delivered services with availability plans}}{\text{Total number of delivered services}} * 100$$

Frequency

    Measured: Monthly

    Reported: Monthly

Acceptable quality level: 99%

    Range: < 99% unacceptable (indicates poor/ incomplete service designs)

                = 99% acceptable (maintain/improve)

                > 99% exceeds (indicates well-designed services)

Note

This AQL allows for one per cent of delivered services to be without an availability plan to account for pipeline activities such as service redesign, service pilots and retiring services.

Metric name
Percentage of incidents caused by unavailability

Metric category
Availability management

Suggested metric owner
Service level manager

Typical stakeholders

IT operations manager, service manager, service desk, customer relationship manager

Description

This measurement provides an indication of the magnitude of issues related to the lack of service availability (unavailability). Depending on the root cause(s) of availability-related incidents, the metric is applied as an indicator of:

- The need for updating the capacity plan
- Unreliable service assets; and/or
- The need for redundant system/subsystem configuration(s) to improve service availability.

The metric can be applied as an input to a Business Impact Analysis (BIA) for service asset unavailability/unreliability.

Measurement description

Formula:

$$\frac{\text{Number of incidents due to availability issues}}{\text{Total number of incidents}} * 100$$

Frequency

Measured: Monthly

Reported: Monthly

Acceptable quality level: 0.05%

Range: > 0.05% unacceptable (indicates unreliable services)

= 0.05% acceptable (maintain/improve)

< 0.05% exceeds (indicates high availability services)

Note

This AQL reflects 99.95% availability of delivered services. This translates to 21.9 minutes per month of unavailability in a 24/7 operating environment. The commonly recognized threshold for a High Availability (HA) system/subsystem is 99.999 ('five nines') which allows for 26.28 seconds per month of unavailability in a 24/7 operating environment. Achieving HA requires investment in redundant service assets to provide the target level of fault tolerance.

Metric name

Percentage of availability threshold alerts

Metric category

Availability management

Suggested metric owner

Service level manager

Typical stakeholders

IT operations manager, service manager, service desk, customer relationship manager

Description

This measurement provides an indication of the magnitude of issues related to monitored service availability (unavailability) thresholds. Depending on the root cause(s) of availability-related alerts, the metric is applied as an indicator of:

- The need for updating the capacity plan
- Evolving patterns of business activity
- Degraded reliability of service assets; and/or
- The need for redundant system/subsystem configuration(s) to sustain service availability.

The metric can be applied as an input to a BIA for service asset unavailability/unreliability.

Measurement description

Formula:

$$\frac{\text{Number of availability threshold alerts}}{\text{Total number of event alerts}} * 100$$

Frequency

> **Measured:**   Monthly

> **Reported:**   Monthly

Acceptable quality level: N/A

> **Range:**   N/A

Set baseline for event alert thresholds; measure and perform trend analysis over time. Expectation for this metric would be a sustained to upward trend from the baseline depending on the service availability, patterns of business activity and service asset lifecycle maturity.

Metric name

Percentage of services that have been tested for availability

Metric category

Availability management

Suggested metric owner

Service level manager

Typical stakeholders

IT operations manager, service manager, change manager, customer relationship manager, customers

Description

This metric demonstrates the successful implementation of the availability testing as part of service release best practices. It shows the percentage of deployed services for which the target availability has been verified through service validation and testing to underpin the defined in SLAs.

The measurement is useful as an indicator of release and deployment management process implementation consistency. The results of this metric should be applied in assessing service delivery risk exposure.

Measurement description

Formula:

$$\frac{\text{Number of delivered services tested for availability}}{\text{Total number of delivered services}} * 100$$

Frequency

> **Measured:** Monthly
>
> **Reported:** Monthly

Acceptable quality level: 99%

> **Range:** < 99% unacceptable (indicates poor/ incomplete service designs)
>
> = 99% acceptable (maintain/improve)
>
> > 99% exceeds (indicates properly deployed services)

Note

This AQL allows for one per cent of services to be implemented without Availability testing. The services for which Availability testing has <u>not</u> been performed should be noted for Service Management risk exposure and identified as Continual Service Improvement (CSI) opportunities.

Metric name

Mean Time Between Failures (MTBF)

Metric category

Availability management

Suggested metric owner

Service level manager

Typical stakeholders

IT operations manager, service level manager, service desk, problem manager, customers

Description

This measurement is a way to describe the availability of a discrete service or service asset. The MTBF expressed as the arithmetic average of the times between service outages/ failures (incidents) as reflected in incident management records.

MTBF is a commonly used measurement for predicting service reliability and is of significant value for:

- Designing service asset configurations to meet the target end-to-end service availability

- Evaluating risks associated with meeting SLAs

- Developing service asset preventive maintenance schedules

- Developing inputs for determining service support staffing levels.

Measurement description

Formula:

$$\frac{\text{Sum (start of down time−start of up time)}}{\text{Total number of service failures}}$$

Frequency

> **Measured:** Monthly
>
> **Reported:** Monthly

Acceptable quality level: N/A

> **Range:** N/A

Set baseline availability target in terms of service outage time (in minutes and/or seconds) per month and per year; measure service incident times and perform MTBF trend analyses over time. Expectation for this metric would be a sustained to upward trend from the baseline depending on the target service availability, preventive maintenance actions, proactive event management and service asset lifecycle maturity.

Metric name

Mean Time Between Service Incidents (MTBSI)

Metric category

Availability management

Suggested metric owner

Service level manager

Typical stakeholders

IT operations manager, service level manager, service desk, problem manager, customers

Description

This measurement is the arithmetic average time from when a service fails, until it next fails. The metric is used for measuring and reporting service reliability and is the equivalent to adding the MTTR, MTRS and MTBF values for a service, as determined from incident management records.

MTBSI is particularly valuable for:

- Measuring and reporting service reliability

- Empirical input to the Service Knowledge Management System (SKMS)
- Identifying CSI opportunities
- Service management decision support.

Measurement description

Formula:

$$MTBSI = MTBF + MTRS$$

Frequency

    Measured: Monthly

    Reported: Monthly

Acceptable quality level: N/A

    Range: N/A

Set baseline availability target in terms of outage time (in minutes and/or seconds) per month and per year; measure failure incident times and perform MTBSI trend analyses over time. Expectation for this metric would be a sustained to upward trend from the baseline depending on the target service availability, preventive maintenance actions, proactive event management and service asset lifecycle maturity.

Metric name

Mean Time to Restore Service (MTRS)

Metric category

Availability management

Suggested metric owner

Service level manager

Typical stakeholders

IT operations manager, service level manager, service desk, problem manager, customers

Description

This metric is the arithmetic average time between implementing action(s) to correct/repair a service failure to the time when the service functionality is restored to the user. The measurement includes service restoration testing and user acceptance times.

The MTRS measurement is valuable for:

- Inputs for service design and ongoing service level management
- Service restoration and user acceptance process assessments
- Evaluating staff skill levels and training needs
- Inputs to the SKMS.

Measurement description

Formula:

Average of the time to repair the service plus the time to restore the service (fully functional).

Frequency

    Measured: Monthly

    Reported: Monthly

Acceptable quality level: N/A

    Range: N/A

Set baseline availability target in terms of outage time (in minutes and/or seconds) per month and per year; capture detailed incident activity times and perform MTRS trend analyses over time. Expectation for this metric would be a sustained to downward trend from the baseline depending on the service asset lifecycle maturity, the maturing technical skills and growth of the SKMS.

Metric name

Mean Time To Repair (MTTR)

Metric category

Availability management

Suggested metric owner

Service level manager

Typical stakeholders

IT operations manager, service level manager, service desk, problem manager, customers

Description

The MTTR measurement is the total time for incident detection, response and corrective action. The metric captured from incident management records and is of significant value for:

- Managing failure recovery times to ensure delivered service levels
- Input for calculating service asset total cost of ownership (TCO)
- Evaluating maintenance staff skill levels and training needs
- Assessing the SKMS
- Service asset lifecycle management decision making (e.g. refresh cycles).

Measurement description

Formula:

Average time between the resolution of an incident and the start of the incident.

Frequency

Measured: Monthly

Reported: Monthly

Acceptable quality level: N/A

    Range: N/A

Set baseline availability target in terms of outage time (in minutes and/or seconds) per month and per year; measure incident corrective action completion times and perform MTTR trend analyses over time. Expectation for this metric would be a sustained to downward trend from the baseline depending on staff technical skills, maturity of the SKMS and the service asset lifecycle maturity.

Metric name

Percentage of services classified as vital business functions

Metric category

Availability management

Suggested metric owner

Service level manager

Typical stakeholders

IT operations manager, service level manager, service desk, problem manager, customers

Description

A vital business function (VBF) is that element of a business process that is critical to the business's success. The more vital a business function is, the higher the target availability that should be inherent to the supporting IT service design. For example, an IT service may support multiple financial management business functions with payroll and accounts receivable as VBFs. This metric is of significant value for:

- Input for ensuring delivered IT services are aligned to needs of the business
- Determining the required service design to meet target availability

- Prioritizing service asset budgets to ensure VBFs are properly supported.

Measurement description

Formula:

$$\frac{\text{Number of IT services classified as VBFs}}{\text{Total number of delivered services}} * 100$$

Frequency

    Measured: Quarterly

    Reported: Semi-annually

Acceptable quality level: N/A

    Range: N/A

Capacity management metrics

The capacity management process focuses on ensuring there is adequate capacity of technical infrastructure and supporting human resources to sustain service delivery within the performance envelope necessary to satisfy SLA targets. Capacity planning considers current and forecasted service demand within such constraints as financial budgets and physical space limits.

Capacity management process metrics provide a profile of service capacity adequacy, indication of service demand trends and performance triggers for service capacity changes. The basic capacity management metrics provided in this section are:

- Percentage of services with capacity plans
- Percentage of incidents caused by capacity issues
- Percentage of alerts caused by capacity issues
- Percentage of RFCs created due to capacity forecasts
- Percentage of services with demand trend reports
- Number of services without capacity thresholds.

Metric name

Percentage of services with capacity plans

Metric category

Capacity management

Suggested metric owner

Capacity manager or service manager

Typical stakeholders

IT operations manager, service level manager, supplier manager, change manager

Description

A viable capacity plan enables sustained delivery of services that meet quality levels prescribed by SLAs. It also provides a sufficient planning timeframe to satisfy projected demand based on patterns of business activity trends and also considers future SLRs for new offerings in the service pipeline.

This metric provides insight into the adequacy of capacity planning and potential risks to meeting SLA obligations. It is also useful for identifying CSI opportunities.

Measurement description

Formula:

$$\frac{\text{Number of services with capacity plans}}{\text{Total number of services}} * 100$$

Frequency

> **Measured:** Quarterly
>
> **Reported:** Quarterly

Acceptable quality level: 99%

> **Range:** < 99% unacceptable (indicates incomplete service design)
>
> = 99% acceptable (maintain/improve)
>
> > 99% exceeds (indicates well-designed services)

Note

This AQL allows for one per cent of delivered services to be without a capacity plan to account for pipeline activities such as service redesign, service pilots and services pending retirement.

Metric name

Percentage of incidents caused by capacity issues

Metric category

Capacity management

Suggested metric owner

Capacity manager or service manager

Typical stakeholders

IT operations manager, service level manager, service desk, problem manager, change manager

Description

This is a measure of service disruptions and/or degradations for which inadequate resource capacity is the root cause. It is important to note that service capacity issues are typically considered in terms of the technical infrastructure components (e.g. transmission bandwidth or storage), but can also involve human resources (i.e. staffing levels for service delivery workloads).

This is a critical metric for demand management. Capacity-driven incidents provide empirical data for continuously assessing the Patterns of Business Activity (PBA) and evaluating service capacity plans. This metric should be captured for each deployed service to support informed decision making.

Measurement description

Formula:

$$\frac{\text{Number of incidents due to service capacity issues}}{\text{Total number of service incidents}} * 100$$

Frequency

Measured: Monthly

Reported: Monthly

Acceptable quality level: N/A

> **Range:** N/A

Set the baseline in accordance with service-specific capacity plan thresholds; measure and perform trend analysis over time. Expectation for this metric would be a sustained to upward trend from the baseline depending on the growth of service utilization and customer PBAs.

Metric name

Percentage of alerts caused by capacity issues

Metric category

Capacity management

Suggested metric owner

Capacity manager or service manager

Typical stakeholders

IT operations manager, service level manager, service desk, problem manager, change manager

Description

This is a *proactive* measurement of service performance based on service capacity issues. It is important to note that service capacity alerts are primarily considered in terms of technical performance thresholds (i.e. event management) although metrics such as labor efficiency variance can provide alerts for service human resource capacity issues (i.e. staffing levels for service delivery workloads).

This is a valuable metric for proactive demand management. Capacity-driven alerts result from continuously monitoring the PBA and comparing service performance to the capacity plan. Capacity alert thresholds should be set for each deployed service to support informed decision making.

Measurement description

Formula:

$$\frac{\text{Number of alerts due to service capacity issues}}{\text{Total number of service alerts}} * 100$$

Frequency

    Measured: Monthly

    Reported: Monthly

Acceptable quality level: N/A

    Range: N/A

Set the service-specific event management threshold baseline in accordance with the capacity plan; measure and perform trend analysis over time. Expectation for this metric would be a sustained to downward trend from the baseline depending on capacity management actions to meet evolving service demand.

Metric name

Percentage of RFCs created due to capacity forecasts

Metric category

Capacity management

Suggested metric owner

Capacity manager or service manager

Typical stakeholders

IT operations manager, service level manager, service desk, problem manager, change manager

Description

This metric provides an indicator of service capacity plan validity. It is based on the need for continuously monitoring demand based on PBAs. The volume of RFCs generated because of capacity utilization trends is an indicator of the effectiveness of the capacity management process and can be used as a trigger for initiating capacity plan updates.

Measurement description

Formula:

$$\frac{\text{Number of RFCs created due to capacity forecasts}}{\text{Total number of RFCs}} * 100$$

Frequency

Measured: Monthly

Reported: Monthly

Acceptable quality level: N/A

Range: N/A

Set the baseline in accordance with utilization projections in the capacity plan; measure and perform trend analysis over time. Expectation for this metric would be a sustained to downward trend from the baseline depending on the evolving accuracy of demand forecasts and the timeliness of capacity plan updates in recognition of patterns of business activity (PBAs).

Metric name

Percentage of services with demand trend reports

Metric category

Capacity management

Suggested metric owner

Capacity manager or service manager

Typical stakeholders

IT operations manager, service level manager, supplier manager, change manager

Description

This metric is closely linked to the 'Percentage of services with capacity plans' and 'Percentage of RFCs created due to capacity forecasts' metrics. It is a high-level profile of capacity management performance efficacy in terms of continuous monitoring, tracking, analyzing and reporting service demand. The measurement is valuable for:

- Evaluating performance of the capacity management process
- Assessing the validity and reliability of capacity utilization forecasts
- Identifying capacity management CSI opportunities.

Measurement description

Formula:

$$\frac{\text{Number of services with demand reports}}{\text{Total number of services}} * 100$$

Frequency

Measured: Monthly

Reported: Monthly

Acceptable quality level: 99%

Range: < 99% unacceptable (indicates incomplete service design)

= 99% acceptable (maintain/improve)

> 99% exceeds (indicates well-designed services)

Note

This AQL allows for one per cent of delivered services to be without demand trend reports to account for pipeline activities such as service redesign, service pilots and services pending retirement.

Metric name

Number of services without capacity thresholds

Metric category

Capacity management

Suggested metric owner

Capacity manager or service manager

Typical stakeholders

IT operations manager, service level manager, supplier manager, change manager

Description

This metric is closely linked to the 'Percentage of alerts caused by capacity issues' metric. It provides insight to the consistency of service capacity management process implementation. The measurement is valuable for:

- Evaluating performance of the capacity management process
- Assessing the level of service risk exposure due to capacity utilization
- Identifying service design CSI opportunities.

Measurement description

Formula: N/A

This is a simple quantitative tally of the delivered services that do not have capacity utilization (i.e. demand management) thresholds established as part of operations performance monitoring.

Frequency

> **Measured:** Monthly

> **Reported:** Monthly

Acceptable quality level: N/A

> **Range:** N/A

Set the baseline in accordance with service design criteria for the capacity management process; measure and perform trend analysis over time. Expectation for this metric would be a sustained to downward trend from the baseline depending on the maturity of capacity management process implementation as part of service design.

IT service continuity management metrics

IT Service Continuity Management (ITSCM) is central to Business Continuity Management (BCM) as an inherent part of risk reduction involving disaster recovery/continuity of operations (DR/COOP) planning. The ITSCM process ensures service designs incorporate the redundancy and recovery options that provide the necessary resilience to meet operational availability established in SLAs.

IT service continuity planning can find business information from a BIA and the level of business risk tolerance for unavailability of the service. A critical element of the ITSCM process is regular verification testing of service continuity plans. The ITSCM metrics presented in this section are:

- Percentage of services with a BIA
- Percentage of services tested for continuity
- Percentage of ITSCM plans aligned to BCM plans
- Number of successful continuity tests
- Percentage of services with continuity plans
- Number of services with annual continuity reviews.

Metric name

Percentage of services with a BIA

Metric category

IT service continuity management

Suggested metric owner

Continuity manager

Typical stakeholders

Customers, management

Description

A BIA provides valuable information to ITSCM and should be performed for, at a minimum, all major services. This analysis will discover all areas of a business service or unit that are critical to the success of the organization. Additionally, the analysis will provide details which outline what and how a potential loss of service and/or data will mean to the business.

This metric will provide an understanding of the services that have an up-to-date BIA which will allow ITSCM to better create contingency plans.

Measurement description

Formula:

$$\frac{\text{Number of services with a BIA}}{\text{Total number of services}} * 100$$

This metric can be collected from within the ITSCM process or through the BCM process.

Frequency

Measured: Quarterly

Reported: Annually

Acceptable quality level: N/A

Range: N/A

Metric name

Percentage of services tested for continuity

Metric category

IT service continuity management

Suggested metric owner

Continuity manager

Typical stakeholders

Customers, management

Description

This quantitative metric allows the organization to understand the volume of services tested during an actual continuity test. There are circumstances when a limited number of services can be tested due to time or resources available. This will assist in the decision making process concerning how many tests to perform each year.

Continuity testing requires detailed planning and commitment from several areas of the organization and must have awareness and support form the highest levels of the organization. Depending on the industry, this metric could become necessary based on government regulations or legislation.

Measurement description

Formula: This first formula measures the services tested compared to only those services with ITSCM plans.

$$\frac{\text{Number of services tested}}{\text{Total number of services with ITSCM plans}} * 100$$

The second formula provides an understanding of tested services as compared to the total number of services offered by the organization.

$$\frac{\text{Number of services tested}}{\text{Total number of services}} * 100$$

These metrics combine to demonstrate the extent of testing performed during the continuity test.

Frequency

Measured: Annually

Reported: Annually

Acceptable quality level: All services with ITSCM plans should be tested at least annually.

Range: Ranges can have a wide dependency based on number and types of tests performed each year.

Metric name

Percentage of ITSCM plans aligned to BCM plans

Metric category

IT service continuity management

Suggested metric owner

Continuity manager

Typical stakeholders

Customers, management

Description

As IT establishes a more business- and service-focus, alignment with the changing business environment is crucial to overall success. For ITSCM, alignment with BCM will ensure that continuity plans will recover both the IT infrastructure and the business services based on business requirements.

This metric will help demonstrate IT's commitment to the business through the alignment of these plans. An important aspect to continuity plans is the BIA, which was mentioned earlier, providing information to closely link IT and business services together.

Measurement description

Formula:

$$\frac{\text{Total ITSCM plans aligned with BCM plans}}{\text{Total number of ITSCM plans}} * 100$$

The metric is on the organization having a BCM function. Many organizations rely on IT to provide this functionality through ITSCM.

Frequency

> **Measured:** Annually
>
> **Reported:** Annually

Acceptable quality level: 100%

> **Range:** If BCM plans are available, IT must align to them.

Metric name

Number of successful continuity tests

Metric category

IT service continuity management

Suggested metric owner

Continuity manager

Typical stakeholders

Customers, management

Description

A previous metric focused on the amount of services tested during a continuity test. This metric helps to understand the success of the test. Continuity tests are performed to demonstrate the organization's ability to recover services in a timely manner during a disaster or crisis. Therefore, successful testing is critical to provide a high level of confidence to customers and stakeholders that, in the event of a disaster, the organization can recover business services.

This metric may be mandatory, based on government regulations or industry standards. A successful test should ultimately be determined by the customer or testing body. This success should be fully documented and certified by management.

Measurement description

Formula: N/A

This metric is a simple tally (count) of the successful tests and can be augmented by a percentage. Evidence of testing should be properly maintained and available for review or audit.

Frequency

Measured: Annually or after testing

Reported: Annually or after testing

Acceptable quality level: N/A

Range: N/A

Metric name

Percentage of services with continuity plans

Metric category

IT service continuity management

Suggested metric owner

Continuity manager

Typical stakeholders

Customers, management

Description

Evidence of continuity plans for all services requiring continuity must be both available for review and up to date based on business requirements. This metric provides management with the information to understand the level of continuity planning and potential readiness.

Based on the type of service provided, or the industry, continuity plans may be required by regulatory bodies. Therefore, this metric provides the information necessary to demonstrate the organization's effort to protect the business from a potential disaster.

Measurement description

Formula:

$$\frac{\text{Number of services with plans}}{\text{Total number of services}} * 100$$

Eventually, all services requiring continuity must have plans that detail:

- Continuity requirements
- Recovery plans
- Resources required
- Timeline (prioritization)
- Stakeholders
- Logistics and facilities.

Frequency

> **Measured:** Annually
>
> **Reported:** Annually

Acceptable quality level: 100%

> **Range:** All selected services must have continuity plans

Metric name

Number of services with annual continuity reviews

Metric category

IT service continuity management

Suggested metric owner

Continuity manager

Typical stakeholders

Customers, management

Description

Continuity reviews should align to continuity testing to ensure that continuity plans meet the requirements of the business. All services should be reviewed to determine:

* If continuity is required
* If continuity plans are still relevant
* If continuity plans are up to date
* If resources are available to support the plans.

This metric provides the assurance that IT is maintaining continuity plans and is protecting the business from potential disaster. Attendees for review meetings include:

* ITSCM personnel
* Business customers
* IT staff members
* Continuity suppliers (vendors)
* Internal audit.

Measurement description

Formula: N/A

This metric is a simple tally (count) of the implemented services with annual service continuity reviews and can be augmented by a percentage. Evidence of review meetings should be captured and stored as part of the overall continuity documentation. This evidence might include:

* Meeting agenda
* Meeting notes
* Attendee list
* Updates to plans.

Frequency

Measured: Annually

Reported: Annually

Acceptable quality level: N/A
    Range: N/A

Information security management metrics

The ISM process is part of the IT governance framework that establishes the directives, policies, practices and responsibilities for protection of information assets from unauthorized access. The purpose of the ISM process is to ensure information is accessed by and/or disclosed to only those with the need and authority to know (confidentiality); information assets are complete, accurate and protected from unauthorized modification (integrity); information is available and usable when needed, the IT systems in which the information resides can resist penetration attacks, and have the fault tolerance to recover from or prevent failures (availability); and the information exchange infrastructure can be trusted (authenticity and non-repudiation). The following ISM process metrics are provided in this section:

- Detection of unauthorized devices
- Detection of unauthorized software
- Secure software/hardware configurations
- Percentage of systems with automatic vulnerability scanning program installed
- Malware defenses implemented
- Application software security measures
- Number of information security audits performed
- Number of security breaches
- Percentage of services with security breaches
- Downtime caused by Denial of Service (DoS) attacks
- Number of DoS threats prevented
- Percentage of services not compliant with patch levels
- Number of network penetration tests conducted
- Percentage of staff with security awareness training
- Percentage of incidents due to security issues
- Percentage of SLAs with security requirements.

Metric name

Detection of unauthorized devices

Metric category

Information security management

Suggested metric owner

Information security manager

Typical stakeholders

IT operations manager, information owners, asset owners

Description

Organizations must first establish information owners and asset owners and their inventory of authorized devices. With the asset inventory assembled, tools pull information from network assets such as switches and routers regarding the machines connected to the network. Whether physical or virtual, each machine directly connected to the network or attached via VPN, currently running or shut down, should be included in an organization's asset inventory.

Measurement description

Formula: N/A

The system must be capable of identifying any new unauthorized devices that are connected to the network within 24 hours. The asset inventory database and alerting system must be able to identify the location, department, and other details of where authorized and unauthorized devices are plugged into the network.

Control test

The evaluation team should connect hardened test systems to at least 10 locations on the network, including a selection of subnets associated with demilitarized zones (DMZs), workstations, and servers. The evaluation team must then verify that the systems generate an alert or e-mail notice regarding the newly connected systems within 24 hours of the test machines being connected to the network.

Frequency

    Measured: Every 12 hours

    Reported: As detection occurs

Acceptable quality level: Automatic detection and isolation of unauthorized system(s) from the network within one hour of the initial alert and send a follow-up alert or e-mail notification when isolation is achieved.

    Range: N/A

Note

While the 24-hour and one-hour timeframes represent the current metric to help organizations improve their state of security, in the future organizations should strive for even more rapid alerting and isolation, with notification about an unauthorized asset connected to the network sent within two minutes and isolation within five minutes.

Metric name

Detection of unauthorized software

Metric category

Information security management

Suggested metric owner

Information security manager

Typical stakeholders

IT operations manager, information owners, software asset owners

Description

The system must be capable of identifying unauthorized software by detecting an attempt to either install or execute it, notifying enterprise administrative personnel within 24 hours through an alert or e-mail. Systems must block installation, prevent execution, or quarantine unauthorized software within one additional hour.

Measurement description

Formula:

Score=100%, if no unauthorized software is found. Minus one per cent for each piece of unauthorized software that is found. Going forward, if the unauthorized software is not removed, score is reduced by two per cent each consecutive month.

Control test

The evaluation team must move a benign software test program that is not included in the authorized software list to 10 systems on the network. The evaluation team must then verify that the systems generate an alert or e-mail regarding the new software within 24 hours.

Frequency

Measured: Monthly

Reported: Monthly

Acceptable quality level: The system must automatically block or quarantine the unauthorized software within one additional hour. The evaluation team must verify that the system provides details of the location of each machine with this new test software, including information about the asset owner.

Range: N/A

Metric name

Secure software/hardware configurations

Metric category

Information security management

Suggested metric owner

Information security manager

Typical stakeholders

IT operations manager, information owners, software asset owners

Description

Organizations can meet this metric by developing a series of images and secure storage servers for hosting these standard images. Commercial and/or free configuration management tools can then be employed to measure the settings for operating systems and applications of managed machines to look for deviations from the standard image configurations used by the organization. File integrity monitoring software is deployed on servers as a part of the base configuration. Centralized solutions like Tripwire® are preferred over stand-alone solutions.

Measurement description

Formula:

A score of 50% is awarded for using an automated tool (e.g. Tripwire®) with a central monitoring/reporting component. The remaining 50% is based on the percentage of servers on which the solution is deployed.

Control test

The evaluation team must move a benign test system that does not contain the official hardened image, but that does contain additional services, ports and configuration file changes, onto the network. This must be performed on 10 different random segments using either real or virtual systems. The evaluation team must then verify that the systems generate an alert or e-mail notice regarding the changes to the software within 24 hours.

Frequency

>   **Measured:**   Monthly

>   **Reported:**   Monthly

Acceptable quality level: 100% (derived per the formula description, above)

The system must automatically block or quarantine the unauthorized software within one additional hour. The evaluation team must verify that the system provides details of the location of each machine with this new test software, including information about the asset owner.

>   **Range:**   N/A

Metric name

Percentage of systems with automatic vulnerability scanning program installed

Metric category

Information security management

Suggested metric owner

Information security manager

Typical stakeholders

IT operations manager, information owners, software asset owners

Description

This metric focuses on continuous security vulnerability assessment and remediation. As vulnerabilities related to unpatched systems are discovered by scanning tools, security personnel should determine and document the amount of time that elapses between the public release of a patch for the system and the occurrence of the vulnerability scan. Tools (e.g. Security Center®, Secunia®, QualysGuard®, *et al*) should be deployed and configured to run automatically.

Measurement description
Formula:

$$\frac{\text{Systems with vulnerability scanning program installed}}{\text{Total number of systems}} * 100$$

Control test

The evaluation team must verify that scanning tools have successfully completed their weekly or daily scans for the previous 30 cycles of scanning, by reviewing archived alerts and reports. If a scan could not be completed in that timeframe, the evaluation team must verify that an alert or e-mail was generated indicating that the scan did not finish.

Frequency
Measured: Daily or weekly

Reported: Monthly

Acceptable quality level: 100% of machines on system running vulnerability scans with patch scores of 95% or higher.

Range: +/- 5% acceptable (daily/weekly patch scores)

Metric name
Malware defenses implemented

Metric category
Information security management

Suggested metric owner
Information security manager

Typical stakeholders

IT operations manager, information owners, software asset owners

Description

Relying on policy and user action to keep anti-malware tools up to date has been widely discredited, as many users have proven incapable of consistently handling this task. To ensure anti-virus signatures are updated, effective organizations use automation. They use the built-in administrative features of enterprise end-point security suites to verify that anti-virus, anti-spyware, and host-based IDS features are active on every managed system.

Measurement description

Formula: The system must identify any malicious software that is installed, attempted to be installed, executed, or attempted to be executed on a computer system within one hour. Determine the per cent of systems that are running anti-virus programs and the per cent of systems that are properly configured and average the two together.

Control test

The evaluation team must move a benign software test program that appears to be malware, such as a European Institute for Computer Anti-virus Research (EICAR) standard anti-virus test file, or benign hacker tools, but that is not included in the official authorized software list to 10 systems on the network via a network share.

Frequency

    Measured: Daily/weekly

    Reported: Monthly

Acceptable quality level: 100% of machines on system running anti-virus software which is configured to run every time a file is opened.

    Range: No range tolerance allowed

Metric name

Application software security measures

Metric category

Information security management

Suggested metric owner

Information security manager

Typical stakeholders

IT operations manager, information owners, software asset owners

Description

Source code testing tools, web application security scanning tools and object code testing tools have proven useful in securing application software, along with manual application of security penetration testing by testers who have extensive programming knowledge and application penetration testing expertise. The Common Weakness Enumeration (CWE) initiative is used by many such tools to identify the weaknesses that they find.

Measurement description

Formula:

- Web Application Firewall (WAF) is installed and functioning: 50 points
- WAF configuration covers the Open Web Application Security Project (OWASP) top 10: 20 points
- WAF configuration defends against top 25 programming errors: 30 points

The system must also be capable of detecting and blocking an application-level software attack attempt, and must generate an alert or send e-mail to enterprise administrative personnel within 24 hours of detection and blocking.

Control test

The evaluation team must use a web application vulnerability scanner to test for each type of flaw identified in the regularly updated list of the *25 Most Dangerous Programming Errors* by Mitre® and the SANS™ Institute. The scanner must be configured to assess all of the organization's Internet-accessible web applications to identify such errors.

Frequency

Measured: Monthly

Reported: Monthly

Acceptable quality level: 100% (verify that WAF is installed between applications and users)

Range: N/A

Metric name

Number of information security audits performed

Metric category

Information security management

Suggested metric owner

Information security manager

Typical stakeholders

IT operations manager, service manager, problem manager, information owners

Description

This metric provides insight to the consistency and maturity of ISM process implementation. The measurement is valuable for:

- Assessing the level of service risk exposure due to security breaches/intrusions

- Evaluating the efficacy of preventive/proactive ISM actions
- Inputs to the design of pipeline services
- Identifying ISM CSI opportunities.

Measurement description

Formula: N/A

This is a simple quantitative tally of the information security audits conducted on delivered service infrastructure assets.

Frequency

> **Measured:** Monthly
>
> **Reported:** Monthly

Acceptable quality level: N/A

> **Range:** N/A

Set the baseline in accordance with service design criteria for the frequency of information security audits as part of the ISM process; measure and perform trend analysis over time. Expectation for this metric would be a sustained to upward trend from the baseline depending on the maturity of implemented ISM process practices, evolving information security threats, number of security breaches and preventive actions necessary to satisfy SLRs.

Metric name

Number of security breaches

Metric category

Information security management

Suggested metric owner

Information security manager

Typical stakeholders

IT operations manager, service manager, problem manager, information owners

Description

This is a high-level forensic (reactive) metric that indicates the effectiveness of information security practices. The measurement is critical to service delivery and is used for:

*   Identifying the need for ISM CSI
*   Assessing the overall level of information security risk exposure
*   Assessment of service ISM staffing levels and skills inventory
*   Inputs to the design of pipeline services
*   Evaluating the efficacy of Intrusion Detection System (IDS) performance.

Measurement description

Formula: N/A

This is a simple quantitative tally of the actual Information Security breaches/intrusions experienced.

Frequency

> **Measured:** Monthly
>
> **Reported:** Monthly

Acceptable quality level: 0

> **Range:** > 0 unacceptable (indicates inadequate information security preventive actions)

Note

This AQL represents a total lack of tolerance for service portfolio information security risk exposure.

Metric name

Percentage of services with security breaches

Metric category

Information security management

Suggested metric owner

Information security manager

Typical stakeholders

IT operations manager, service manager, service desk, problem manager, information owners

Description

This metric is a forensic (reactive) indicator of the effectiveness of information security across the service portfolio. The measurement is critical to overall service management and is used for:

- Assessing the level of service portfolio risk exposure due to security breaches/intrusions
- Evaluating the efficacy of ISM proactive/preventive actions
- Evaluating the efficacy of IDS performance
- Assessment of service ISM staffing levels and skills inventory
- Inputs to the design of pipeline services
- Identifying ISM CSI opportunities.

Measurement description

Formula:

$$\frac{\text{Number of services with security breaches}}{\text{Total number of services}} * 100$$

Frequency

Measured: Daily

Reported: Weekly

Acceptable quality level: 0%

Range: > 0% unacceptable (indicates inadequate information security preventive actions)

Note

This AQL reflects a total lack of tolerance for service portfolio Information Security risk exposure.

Metric name

Downtime caused by Denial of Service (DoS) attacks

Metric category

Information security management

Suggested metric owner

Information security manager

Typical stakeholders

IT operations manager, service level manager, service desk, problem manager, customers

Description

This is an ISM forensic metric derived from root cause analysis of Security incidents. The measurement is valuable for:

- Assessing IDS alert thresholds and overall performance
- Assessing the service level risk exposure from DoS attacks
- Evaluating ISM CSI opportunities.

Measurement description

Formula: N/A

This is a simple quantitative tally of the actual downtime experienced from DoS attacks.

Frequency

> **Measured:** Daily
>
> **Reported:** Weekly

Acceptable quality level: 0

> **Range:** > 0 unacceptable (indicates inadequate information security preventive actions)

Note

This AQL reflects a total lack of tolerance for service portfolio information security risk exposure.

Metric name

Number of DoS threats prevented

Metric category

Information security management

Suggested metric owner

Information security manager

Typical stakeholders

IT operations manager, service desk, service level manager, problem manager, customers

Description

This metric provides an indication of ISM process and practices effectiveness. The measurement is valuable for:

- Assessing the service level risk exposure from DoS attacks
- Evaluating the efficacy of IDS performance
- Evaluating the efficacy of ISM proactive/preventive actions

- Input to valuation of ISM in terms of availability.

Measurement description

Formula: N/A

This is a simple quantitative tally of DoS threats prevented (i.e. DoS attacks thwarted).

Frequency

 Measured: Daily

 Reported: Weekly

Acceptable quality level: N/A

 Range: N/A

Set the baseline availability in accordance with service design criteria; measure and perform trend analysis over time. Expectation for this metric would be a sustained to downward trend from the baseline depending on the maturity of implemented ISM practices, evolving information security threats, IDS thresholds and ISM preventive actions necessary to meet SLRs.

Metric name

Percentage of services not compliant with patch levels

Metric category

Information security management

Suggested metric owner

Information security manager

Typical stakeholders

IT operations manager, service level manager, service desk, problem manager, change manager

Description

This metric provides an indicator of implemented ISM preventive actions as part of meeting SLRs. The measurement is significant to overall service management and is used for:

- Assessing the level of service portfolio risk exposure due to security breaches/intrusions
- Evaluating the efficacy of ISM proactive/preventive actions
- Assessment of service ISM workloads, staffing levels and skills inventory
- Inputs to the design of pipeline services
- Identifying ISM CSI opportunities.

Measurement description

Formula:

$$\frac{\text{Number of services not compliant with patch levels}}{\text{Total number of services}} * 100$$

Frequency

> **Measured:** Weekly
>
> **Reported:** Weekly

Acceptable quality level: 0%

> **Range:** > 0% unacceptable (indicates inadequate information security preventive actions)

Note

This AQL reflects a total lack of tolerance for service portfolio information security risk exposure.

Metric name

Number of network penetration tests conducted

Metric category

Information security management

Suggested metric owner

Information security manager

Typical stakeholders

IT operations manager, service level manager, problem manager, information owners

Description

This metric provides an indication of ISM process and proactive/preventive actions. The measurement is valuable for:

- Assessing the level of service portfolio risk exposure due to security breaches/intrusions
- Evaluating the efficacy of ISM proactive/preventive actions
- Assessment of service ISM workloads, staffing levels and skills inventory.

Measurement description

Formula: N/A

This is a simple quantitative tally of network penetration tests conducted as part of the ISM standard practices.

Frequency

> **Measured:** Monthly

> **Reported:**   Monthly

Acceptable quality level: N/A

> **Range:**   N/A

Set the baseline number and frequency for network penetration testing in accordance with ISM policies;

measure and perform trend analysis over time. Expectation for this metric would be a sustained to upward trend from the baseline depending on the maturity of implemented ISM practices, evolving information security threats, IDS thresholds and ISM preventive actions necessary to meet SLRs.

Metric name

Percentage of staff with security awareness training

Metric category

Information security management

Suggested metric owner

Information security manager

Typical stakeholders

IT operations manager, service manager, service desk, change manager

Description

This metric is an indicator of implemented ISM practices. Security awareness training is an inherent part of preventing security breaches from internal sources and making each staff member accountable for the security implications of his/her actions. The measurement is valuable for:

- Reducing the level of service portfolio risk exposure due to internal security breaches
- Assessing staff training needs
- Identifying ISM CSI opportunities.

Measurement description

Formula:

$$\frac{\text{Number of staff with security awareness training}}{\text{Total number of staff}} * 100$$

Frequency

> **Measured:** Monthly
>
> **Reported:** Monthly

Acceptable quality level: 100%

> **Range:** < 100% unacceptable (indicates security awareness training gaps)
>
> = 100% acceptable (indicates properly implemented security awareness training program)

Note

This AQL is intended to make security awareness a high priority for the service provider as part of sustaining the integrity of delivered services.

Metric name

Percentage of incidents due to security issues

Metric category

Information security management

Suggested metric owner

Information security manager

Typical stakeholders

IT operations manager, service desk, service level manager, problem manager, change manager

Description

This metric provides an indicator of the magnitude of information security issues as part of service support. The measurement is used for:

- Evaluating the efficacy of ISM proactive/preventive actions
- Assessment of service ISM workloads and staffing levels

- Identifying service desk CSI opportunities (e.g. pre-approved changes, incident escalation times, etc.)
- Assessing service desk workloads, staffing levels and skills inventory
- Identifying ISM CSI opportunities.

Measurement description

Formula: N/A

Frequency

    Measured: Monthly

    Reported: Monthly

Acceptable quality level: N/A

    Range: N/A

Set the baseline in accordance with service desk, ISM and change management criteria; measure and perform trend analysis over time. Expectation for this metric would be a sustained to downward trend from the baseline depending on the SKMS maturity, evolving information security threats, and ISM preventive actions.

Metric name

Percentage of SLAs with security requirements

Metric category

Information security management

Suggested metric owner

Information security manager

Typical stakeholders

IT operations manager, service level manager, service desk, customers

Description

This metric is provides an indicator of SLM process maturity. The measurement is used for:

- Identifying service design CSI opportunities
- Evaluating SLA updates.

Measurement description

Formula:

$$\frac{\text{Number of SLAs with security requirements}}{\text{Total number of SLAs}} * 100$$

Frequency

Measured: Monthly

Reported: Monthly

Acceptable quality level: 99%

Range: < 99% unacceptable (indicates incomplete SLAs)

= 99% acceptable (maintain/improve)

> 99% exceeds (indicates mature SLAs)

Note

This AQL allows for one per cent of the SLAs to be without security requirements to account for pipeline activities such as service redesign, service pilots and services pending retirement.

Supplier management metrics

The supplier management process ensures suppliers and their delivered products and services meet IT service level targets and business expectations. Supplier management efforts are focused on ensuring that underpinning contracts (UCs) and agreements with suppliers are aligned with the business needs and suppliers meet their commitments.

The supplier management process encompasses managing the suppliers and contracts to seamlessly support delivery of IT services to the business. The metrics provided in this section are:

- Percentage of contracts reviewed annually
- Percentage of suppliers with a supplier manager
- Number of suppliers using sub-contractors
- Number of contracts with breached targets
- Number of SCMIS audits performed
- Number of new suppliers added
- Number of contracts terminated
- Number of contracts aligned to an SLA.

Metric name

Percentage of contracts reviewed annually

Metric category

Supplier management

Suggested metric owner

Supplier manager

Typical stakeholders

Customers, management, suppliers (vendors), financial management, contract management

Description

This metric provides an understanding of the level that suppliers and contracts are managed. Actively reviewing and working with suppliers builds a stronger relationship between the provider and supplier while ensuring the terms of the contract are being met and in line with the SLA targets. Reviews should be formally scheduled with the supplier via meetings, conference calls, video conference or other interactive mediums.

These reviews allow the opportunity for both parties to share current and future activities that might have an impact to the contract and proactively plan for changes to keep the contract relevant to the supported services. Results from these reviews can then be shared during the SLA reviews.

Measurement description

Formula:

$$\frac{\text{Number of contracts reviewed annually}}{\text{Total number of contracts}} * 100$$

This metric can be measured via calendars, meeting notes and other artifacts that provide evidence of the review.

Frequency

Measured: Quarterly

Reported: Annually

Acceptable quality level: All contracts should be reviewed annually

Range: N/A

Metric name

Percentage of suppliers with a supplier manager

Metric category

Supplier management

Suggested metric owner

Supplier manager

Typical stakeholders

Management, suppliers (vendors), contract management

Description

Suppliers and contracts must be actively managed to ensure quality and value are achieved for the customers. Therefore, suppliers must have a supplier manager assigned to oversee the deliverables provided by the supplier.

Assigning a supplier manager provides benefits such as:

- Improved supplier relationships
- Improved service delivery
- Alignment with SLAs and OLAs
- Increased knowledge sharing with suppliers
- Vendor giveaways (shirts, coffee mugs, pens, etc.).

Measurement description

Formula:

$$\frac{\text{Number of suppliers with supplier manager}}{\text{Total number of suppliers}} * 100$$

This metric is collected manually and should be monitored to ensure the proper management of suppliers.

Frequency

Measured: Quarterly

Reported: Annually

Acceptable quality level: All suppliers should have a supplier manager assigned.
Range: N/A

Metric name

Number of suppliers using sub-contractors

Metric category

Supplier management

Suggested metric owner

Supplier manager

Typical stakeholders

Customers, management, IT staff, supplier (vendors), financial management, contract management

Description

The use of sub-contractors increases the overall value brought to the service provider from the supplier. Managing sub-contractors is the responsibility of the supplier but the service provider must still understand which of the suppliers are using subs in the provision of products and services.

This metric provides that level of understanding and keeps the provider abreast of the number of subs being used. This becomes important when trying to ensure the appropriate level of value is being achieved for the money spent.

Measurement description

Formula:

$$\frac{\text{Total number of suppliers using subs}}{\text{Total number of suppliers}} * 100$$

The metric can be presented as percentage or as a straight number depending on the organization's preference. Monitor this metric closely and regularly watching the depth of the sub-contractor chain as value can decrease as more subs are added to the chain.

- Supplier
  - ○ Sub-contractor
    - ○ Sub-contractor
      - ○ Sub-contractor

Frequency

> **Measured:** Quarterly
>
> **Reported:** Annually

Acceptable quality level: N/A

> **Range:** N/A

Metric name

Number of contracts with breached targets

Metric category

Supplier management

Suggested metric owner

Supplier manager

Typical stakeholders

Customers, management, IT staff, supplier (vendors), financial management, contract management

Description

A breached contract is a situation which no one wants to have happen. If a contract target is missed or the supplier fails to perform properly the contract can be viewed as being in a breached state which is a losing scenario for all parties. In many cases, the service provider's level of service is only as good as their supplier's performance.

This metric demonstrates the ongoing monitoring of contracts as supplier management strives to ensure the highest level of delivery from the suppliers. If this situation does occur it is to the benefit of all parties that it is captured and managed quickly to minimize the adverse impact of the breach.

Measurement description

Formula: N/A

This is a simple quantitative tally. Regular tracking of this metric can help discover patterns of execution by suppliers and identify opportunities to repair these breached targets.

Frequency

>**Measured:**   Weekly

>**Reported:**   Monthly

Acceptable quality level: Set a baseline and monitor

>**Range:**   0 breaches within the reporting period

Metric name

Number of SCMIS audits performed

Metric category

Supplier management

Suggested metric owner

Supplier manager

Typical stakeholders

Customers, management, IT staff, supplier (vendors), financial management, contract management

Description

The Supplier and Contract Management Information System (SCMIS) is the central repository for all documents and information related to supplier management and the suppliers.

This metric will provides a level of certainty of the quality and accuracy of the information found in the SCMIS. Audit points of interest can include:

- Quality and accuracy of information
- Up-to-date documentation
- Number of accesses to the SCMIS
- Who has access?
- Backup information
- Number of managed changes.

Measurement description

Formula: N/A

This is a simple tally (count). While number of audits might be a small number, it is still important to monitor this metric to ensure the highest level of quality.

Frequency

> **Measured:** Annually

> **Reported:** Annually

Acceptable quality level: 1 audit per year

> **Range:**   < 1 unacceptable

> = 1 acceptable

> > 1 exceed

Metric name

Number of new suppliers added

Metric category

Supplier management

Suggested metric owner

Supplier manager

Typical stakeholders

Customers, management, IT staff, supplier (vendors), financial management, contract management

Description

This metric helps monitor and understand the growth of the organization's supplier base. There are several activities involved with bringing a new supplier on board. These might include:

- Assigning a supplier manager
- Linking the contract to other agreements (SLAs/OLAs)
- Establishing the supplier within the organization
- Setting up financial systems.

Having the knowledge provided by this metric will assist management with resource planning and understanding the time required to get this new supplier fully engrained within the organization.

Measurement description

Formula: N/A

This metric can be combined with other metrics to demonstrate the amount of activity required to properly bring a new supplier into the organization.

Frequency

    Measured: Quarterly

    Reported: Annually

Acceptable quality level: N/A

    Range: N/A

Metric name

Number of contracts terminated

Metric category

Supplier management

Suggested metric owner

Supplier manager

Typical stakeholders

Customers, management, IT staff, supplier (vendors), financial management, contract management

Description

This metric provides an understanding of supplier turnover. At times, this turnover can create disruption within the organization as the services and products provided by the supplier might no longer be available. This could be compounded by the addition of a new supplier to replace the outgoing supplier. Reasons for termination include:

- Contract breaches
- Supplier performance
- End of life for the contract
- Products or services no longer required.

Measurement description

Formula: N/A

This metric can be combined with the previous metric (Number of new suppliers added) to provide a clear picture of supplier activity and turnover.

Frequency

    Measured: Quarterly

    Reported: Annually

Acceptable quality level: N/A

    Range: N/A

Metric name

Number of contracts aligned to an SLA

Metric category

Supplier management

Suggested metric owner

Supplier manager

Typical stakeholders

Customers, management, IT staff, supplier (vendors), financial management, contract management

Description

This metric can help show the purpose for a supplier. Contracts must be reviewed regularly to ensure they facilitate and benefit the services to the customers. Maintaining alignment with an SLA will also ensure that updates and improvements will provide direct impact to the service and potentially increase the value of the product or service provided by the supplier.

Monitoring the alignment between an SLA and a contract will increase the value proposition for all parties involved and can strengthen the relationship between the service provider and the supplier.

Measurement description

Formula: N/A

This metric will demonstrate the proactive activities of supplier management to ensure the value and viability of the contract and supplier.

Frequency

> **Measured:** Quarterly
>
> **Reported:** Quarterly

Acceptable quality level: N/A

> **Range:** N/A

CHAPTER 5: SERVICE TRANSITION METRICS

Service transition provides guidance on effectively managing the transition of design services into a delivered operational state. Transition management ensures a disciplined, repeatable approach for implementing new and changed services to minimize quality/technical, schedule and cost risk exposure. It helps ensure new and changed services are delivered with the complete functionality prescribed by the service strategy requirements and built into the service design package.

Service transition processes and metrics are used throughout the service lifecycle as part of sustaining service delivery to meet business needs. The metrics in this chapter are linked to the Critical Success Factors (CSFs) and KPIs established for service transition processes. The metrics sections for this chapter are:

Transition planning and support metrics

Change management metrics

Service asset and configuration management metrics

Release and deployment management metrics

Service validation and testing metrics

Change evaluation metrics

Knowledge management metrics.

Transition planning and support metrics

The metrics in this section support the transition planning and support process. These metrics are in line with the KPIs identified for this process. The metrics presented in this section are:

- Percentage of releases that meet customer requirements
- Percentage of service transitions from RFCs
- Percentage of new or changed services implemented.

Metric name

Percentage of releases that meet customer requirements

Metric category

Transition planning and support

Suggested metric owner

Release manager

Typical stakeholders

IT operations manager, service level manager, service desk, configuration manager

Description

This is a measure of the number of implemented releases that meet the customer's agreed requirements in terms of scope (functionality), quality, cost and release schedule – as a percentage of all releases.

Measurement description

Formula:

$$\frac{\text{Releases without scope, quality, cost, or schedule variance}}{\text{Total number of releases deployed}} * 100$$

Frequency

Measured: Monthly

Reported: Monthly

Acceptable quality level: +/- 5% Variance from agreed requirements

Range: > +/- 5% unacceptable (transition possibly out of control)

= 95% to 105% of requirements acceptable (maintain/improve)

< +/- 5% exceeds (indicates a well-managed transition)

Metric name

Percentage of service transitions from RFCs

Metric category

Transition planning and support

Suggested metric owner

Change manager

Typical stakeholders

IT operations manager, service level manager, configuration manager

Description

This is a measure for assessing the volume of service changes implemented as a result of requests for change (RFCs). It is expressed in terms of the ratio (percentage) of service changes implemented to the total number of services in operation.

Measurement description

Formula:

$$\frac{\text{Number of service changes implemented}}{\text{Total number of services in operation}} * 100$$

Frequency

    Measured: Monthly

    Reported: Quarterly

Acceptable quality level: N/A

    Range: NA

Set baseline percentage of service transitions based on RFCs; measure and perform trend analysis over time. Expectation for this metric would be a sustained to upward trend from the baseline.

Note

This metric relates only to those new or changed services that have been created as a result of RFC submissions. RFCs may also be generated and approved as part of Release and deployment management (RDM) process for transitioning new or changed services into operations.

Metric name

Percentage of new or changed services implemented

Metric category

Transition planning and support

Suggested metric owner

Change manager

Typical stakeholders

IT operations manager, information security manager, capacity manager, configuration manager

Description

This is a measure for assessing the volume of services transition efforts, as a percentage of the combined total of all operational services. The metric provides an indicator of the workloads and service transition process activity levels.

Measurement description

Formula:

$$\frac{\text{Number of new or changed services transitioned}}{\text{Total number of services in operation}} * 100$$

Frequency

> **Measured:** Monthly
>
> **Reported:** Quarterly

Acceptable quality level: N/A

Range: N/A

Set baseline percentage of new or changed services implemented in the period; measure and perform trend analysis over time. The expectation for this metric would be a sustained to upward trend from the baseline.

Change management metrics

Change management metrics are of significant value as indicators of process maturity and potential improvement opportunities. The metric calculations provided in this section directly correlate to the KPIs identified for this process. The metrics presented in this section are:

- Percentage of emergency changes
- Percentage of standard changes
- Percentage of successful changes
- Percentage of changes that cause incidents
- Percentage of rejected changes
- Change backlog
- Percentage of backed out changes (remediation plan invoked)
- Unauthorized changes
- Percentage of failed changes
- Percentage of changes completed with no errors/issues.

Metric name

Percentage of emergency changes

Metric category

Change management

Suggested metric owner

Change manager

Typical stakeholders

Change submitter, service desk, other ITSM functions

Description

This metric represents the percentage of emergency changes in the environment (production, UAT, pilot, etc.).

This downward trending metric can demonstrate issues in the infrastructure, with software or abuse of the process. Emergency changes can have a direct correlation to incidents and, therefore, must be defined properly to minimize confusion between the two.

After the initial implementation of change management, there is a tendency to see a high percentage of emergency changes in the environment. This can be caused by unfamiliarity with the process and change types or the potential of abuse as changes are pushed through without regard for the normal process and timeline (getting around the process).

Measurement description

This measurement should be gathered within a defined timeframe (i.e. monthly, quarterly). It is recommended that during the early stages of the change management process this metric be reviewed on a weekly basis to prevent abuse of proper categorization.

Formula:

$$\frac{\text{Number of emergency changes}}{\text{Total number of closed changes}} * 100$$

Frequency

    Measured: Weekly

    Reported: Monthly

Acceptable quality level: 5%

    Range: > 5% unacceptable (improvement opportunity)

                  = 5% acceptable (maintain/improve)

                  < 5% exceeds (process maturity level 4-5 potential)

Metric name

Percentage of standard changes

Metric category

Change management

Suggested metric owner

Change manager

Typical stakeholders

Change submitter, service desk, other ITSM functions

Description

This metric represents the percentage of standard (pre-approved) changes in the environment (production, UAT, pilot, etc.). This is an upward trending metric that, if used properly, makes simple changes more efficient within the process. We recommend setting a rather aggressive goal for this metric and look to move a majority of changes to a standard change type as many changes are low risk operational changes.

This type of change should grow as the change management process matures. As change management rolls out, standard changes are usually not prevalent in the environment. Low risk, highly successful changes will begin to emerge which should then be taken through a procedure to qualify as a documented standard change.

Measurement description

Formula:

$$\frac{\text{Number of standard changes}}{\text{Total number of closed changes}} * 100$$

This measurement should be gathered within a defined timeframe (i.e. monthly, quarterly). It is recommended that during the early stages of the change management process this metric be review on a monthly basis.

Frequency

> **Measured:** Weekly
>
> **Reported:** Monthly

Acceptable quality level: Set an aggressive level such as 60% realizing this is a medium-term goal

> **Range:** < 60% unacceptable (improvement opportunity)
>
> = 60% acceptable (maintain/improve)
>
> > 60% exceeds (review to consider resetting goal)

Metric name

Percentage of successful changes

Metric category

Change management

Suggested metric owner

Change manager

Typical stakeholders

Change submitter, service desk, other ITSM functions, IT management

Description

This metric represents the percentage of successful changes in the environment (production, UAT, pilot, etc.). While all organizations would prefer to have this metric at 100%, the reality is that things happen (i.e. hardware failure, software incompatibility, human error) which prevent success for all changes. It is that reality which brings light to the fact that due diligence must be taken for all changes in order to establish high levels of success.

It is important to note that change management process maturity evolves over time through lessons learned. It is expected that this metric will show an upward trend in successful changes as an indicator of the acceptance and maturity of change management in the environment.

Measurement description
Formula:

$$\frac{\text{Number of successful changes}}{\text{Total number of closed changes}} * 100$$

This measurement should be gathered within a defined timeframe (i.e. monthly, quarterly). When combined with a downward trending incident number, this will demonstrate improved levels of service for the entire organization.

Frequency

Measured: Weekly

Reported: Monthly

Acceptable quality level: 98%

Range: < 98% unacceptable (improvement opportunity)

= 98% acceptable (maintain/improve)

> 98% exceeds (process maturity level 4-5 potential)

Metric name
Percentage of changes that cause incidents

Metric category
Change management

Suggested metric owner
Change manager

Typical stakeholders

Change submitter, service desk, operations manager

Description

This metric represents the percentage of changes in the environment (production, UAT, pilot, etc.) which have directly caused an incident to be created. This must be a downward trending metric exhibiting improvement in all aspects of change and the execution of the change management process.

The relationship between changes and incidents can be created and tracked through many IT service management tools found in the marketplace. This relationship should be established early in the development and deployment of the tool.

Measurement description

Formula:

$$\frac{\text{Number of change-related incidents}}{\text{Total number of closed changes}} * 100$$

This metric should be gathered in a pre-defined timeframes (e.g. weekly or monthly).

Frequency

> **Measured:** Weekly
>
> **Reported:** Monthly

Acceptable quality level: 3%

> **Range:** > 3% unacceptable (improvement opportunity)
>
> = 3% acceptable (maintain/improve)
>
> < 3% exceeds (process maturity level 4-5 potential)

Metric name

Percentage of rejected changes

Metric category

Change management

Suggested metric owner

Change manager, Change Advisory Board (CAB)

Typical stakeholders

Change submitter

Description

This metric represents the percentage of rejected changes through the process execution. As changes are reviewed within the change management process, either the change manager or the CAB will determine if the change should be rejected. This metric can reveal both the awareness and understanding of the change management process by understanding the reason behind the rejection.

There are multiple reasons for rejecting a change, most commonly due to missing information within the change record or scheduling conflicts.

Measurement description

Formula:

$$\frac{\text{Number of rejected changes}}{\text{Total number of closed changes}} * 100$$

This measurement should be gathered in pre-defined timeframes (e.g. weekly or monthly).

Frequency

Measured: Weekly

Reported: Monthly

Acceptable quality level: 2%

Range: > 2% unacceptable (improvement or training opportunity)

= 2% acceptable (maintain/improve)

< 2% exceeds (process maturity level 4-5 potential)

Metric name

Change backlog

Metric category

Change management

Suggested metric owner

Change manager

Typical stakeholders

Change submitter, service desk, operations manager, service level management, business customers

Description

This metric represents the number of changes creating a change backlog. A backlog can be created by a number issues or reasons including:

- Pending – changes requiring additional information, resources or authorization
- Postponed – changes put on hold due to business or scheduling conflicts
- Rejected – rejected via assessment and review
- Waiting for approval – changes in the process and waiting for final approval.

The change backlog can be managed within an ITSM tool and should be reviewed during the CAB meeting. The backlog should be reported by time (i.e. days or weeks in the backlog).

Measurement description

Formula: N/A

It is simply reported as the number of changes backlogged and the length of time in the backlog queue.

This measurement should be gathered within a defined timeframe (i.e. monthly or quarterly). A high number of backlogged changes can be a sign of issues within the change management process or with management decision making.

Frequency

> **Measured:**   Weekly
>
> **Reported:**   Monthly

Acceptable quality level: Maximum backlog queue determined by IT management

> **Range:**   N/A

Metric name

Percentage of backed out changes (remediation plan invoked)

Metric category

Change management

Suggested metric owner

Change manager

Typical stakeholders

Change submitter, service desk, IT management, service level management, customers

Description

This metric represents the percentage of changes that were implemented or partially implemented but needed to be backed out due to issues with the change. This metric can demonstrate value of remediation plans showing timely decision making and execution within the given change window. No change should be approved without a pre-defined remediation plan included.

To properly create the time for a change window, change management will consider the time required to implement the change and the time required to implement a back out. This ensures the decision to back out can be made within the change window thus minimizing the impact and/or outage to the service and business.

Measurement description

Formula:

$$\frac{\text{Number of backed out changes}}{\text{Total number of closed changes}} * 100$$

This measurement should be gathered pre-defined timeframes (e.g. weekly or monthly).

Frequency

> **Measured:** Weekly
>
> **Reported:** Monthly

Acceptable quality level: 5%

> **Range:** > 5% unacceptable (improvement opportunity)
>
> = 5% acceptable (maintain/improve)
>
> < 5% exceeds (process maturity level 4-5 potential)

Metric name

Unauthorized changes

Metric category

Change management

Suggested metric owner

Change manager

Typical stakeholders

Service desk, IT management, service level management, customers

Description

This number represents a serious breach of process protocol and must not be tolerated. Detecting unauthorized changes can be difficult based on the tools or resources available to research these activities. Means of detection include:

* Tools — tools that can monitor and report changes within the environment

* CMDB audits — compare differences in the CMDB to change records

* Server log audits — research activities recorded in log files and compare against change records.

A large number of issues can result from unauthorized changes which can create severe delays in incident and problem management. This increases the downtime of services and jeopardizes the overall reliability and quality of the service.

Measurement description

Formula: N/A

This number should be gathered within a defined timeframe (i.e. weekly, monthly).

Frequency

> **Measured:** Weekly

> **Reported:** Monthly

Acceptable quality level: 0

> **Range:** N/A

Metric name

Percentage of failed changes

Metric category

Change management

Suggested metric owner

Change manager

Typical stakeholders

Change submitter, service desk, IT management

Description

This metric represents the percentage of failed changes in the environment (production, UAT, pilot, etc.). This downward trending metric can demonstrate issues in the change planning, change activities, the infrastructure or with conflicting changes. Failed changes must be clearly defined within the change management process as these can include several instances such as complete failures, back outs, partial failures or change conflict/collision.

Measurement description

Formula:

$$\frac{\text{Number of failed changes}}{\text{Total number of closed changes}} * 100$$

This measurement should be gathered within a defined timeframe (i.e. monthly, quarterly).

Frequency

    Measured: Weekly

    Reported: Monthly

Acceptable quality level: 5%

    Range: > 5% unacceptable (improvement opportunity)

                = 5% acceptable (maintain/improve)

< 5% exceeds (process maturity level 4-5 potential)

Metric name

Percentage of changes completed with no errors/issues

Metric category

Change management

Suggested metric owner

Change manager

Typical stakeholders

IT operations manager, change manager, configuration manager, service level manager, service desk

Description

This metric represents the number of changes that have been implemented successfully the first time as planned, without executing a back out or incurring any errors from verification testing.

Measurement description

Formula:

$$\frac{\text{Number of changes implemented with no errors}}{\text{Total number of closed changes}} * 100$$

Frequency

Measured: Monthly

Reported: Monthly

Acceptable quality level: 95%

Range: < 95% unacceptable (service asset management possibly out of control)

= 95% acceptable (maintain/improve)

> 95% exceeds (indicates service
> assets are well-managed)

Note

This AQL allows incurring errors/issues with up to five per cent of the implemented changes due to conditions in the implementation environment and other risk factors.

Service asset and configuration management metrics

Configuration management metrics are of significant value as indicators of process maturity and potential improvement opportunities. The metrics in this section reflect the CSFs and KPIs identified for Service Asset and Configuration Management (SACM). It is important to note that these are not intended as the definitive set of possible SACM process metrics. As for all processes, the metrics applied must support decisions based on alignment to the business. The metrics presented in this section are:

- Percentage of audited configuration items (CIs)
- Percentage of CIs mapped to IT services in the CMDB
- Average age of IT hardware assets
- Percentage of CIs with maintenance contracts
- Percentage of recorded changes to the CMDB
- Percentage of accurately registered CIs in CMDB.

Metric name

Percentage of audited CIs

Metric category

Service asset and configuration management

Suggested metric owner

Configuration manager

Typical stakeholders

Configuration manager, service desk, IT operations manager

Description

This measurement monitors the number of deployed CIs with an audit date in a given time period relative to the total number of all deployed CIs. Regular audits of the CMDB are important as a quality assurance activity to ensure the CI information is accurate and up to date.

Measurement description

Formula:

$$\frac{\text{Number of CIs audited}}{\text{Total number of CIs}} * 100$$

Frequency

Measured: Quarterly

Reported: Quarterly

Acceptable quality level: 95%

Range: < 95% unacceptable (improvement opportunity)

= 95% acceptable (maintain/improve)

> 95% exceeds (process maturity level 4 or 5 potential)

Metric name

Percentage of CIs mapped to IT services in the CMDB

Metric category

Service asset and configuration management

Suggested metric owner

Configuration manager

Typical stakeholders

Configuration manager, IT operations manager, other ITSM functions

Description

This measurement shows the magnitude of CIs mapped to IT services in the CMDB relative to all CIs comprising the delivered IT services.

This metric is useful as an indicator of the magnitude of CI investments that are related to supporting organizational operations and other functions not directly related to delivering services.

Measurement description

Formula:

$$\frac{\text{Number of CIs mapped to services in CMDB}}{\text{Total number of service asset CIs}} * 100$$

Frequency

Measured: Quarterly

Reported: Quarterly

Acceptable quality level: 95%

Range: < 95% unacceptable (improvement opportunity)

= 95% acceptable (maintain/improve)

> 95% exceeds (process maturity level 4 or 5 potential)

Metric name

Average age of IT hardware assets

Metric category

Service asset and configuration management

Suggested metric owner

Asset manager

Typical stakeholders

Configuration manager, IT operations manager, other ITSM functions

Description

The average age of hardware assets documented and managed as CIs provides a high-level indicator of IT hardware obsolescence with the related issues of maintenance costs to sustain availability and reliability targets. The results of this measurement are a valuable input for IT asset investment decision making as well as for assessing service risks.

Measurement description

Formula:

$$\frac{\text{Total age of IT hardware assets}}{\text{Total number of IT hardware assets}}$$

Frequency

Measured: Quarterly

Reported: Quarterly

Acceptable quality level: 5 years

Range: > 5 years unacceptable (potential risks to operational integrity)

= 5 years or less acceptable (sustainable IT investments)

Metric name

Percentage of CIs with maintenance contracts

Metric category

Service asset and configuration management

Suggested metric owner

Configuration manager

Typical stakeholders

Configuration manager, service desk, IT operations manager, service level manager, customers

Description

This measurement monitors the number of deployed CIs that are within their warranty service period or are related to a valid maintenance contract, relative to the total number of deployed CIs.

This is an indicator of CI maintenance support sources and the associated considerations for establishing SLAs. This metric also provides an indicator of internal maintenance staffing workloads as well as a profile of reliability risk transference.

Measurement description

Formula:

$$\frac{\text{Number of CIs with maintenance contracts}}{\text{Total number of service asset CIs}}$$

Frequency

> **Measured:** Monthly

> **Reported:** Monthly

Acceptable quality level: 99%

> **Range:** < 99% unacceptable (service asset management possibly out of control)
>
> = 99% acceptable (maintain/improve)
>
> > 99% exceeds (indicates service assets are well managed)

Note

This AQL allows for up to one per cent of all deployed service assets to be without an underpinning maintenance support agreement. As an example, maintenance support may not be required for CIs associated with a service that is being retired.

Metric name

Percentage of recorded changes to the CMDB

Metric category

Service asset and configuration management

Suggested metric owner

Configuration manager

Typical stakeholders

IT operations manager, change manager, configuration manager, service level manager, service desk

Description

This metric indicates the magnitude of changes to the CMDB records in a specific reporting period. The measurement provides high-level insight to the magnitude of change activities, and supports trend analyses associated with service delivery workloads and patterns of business activity.

Measurement description

Formula:

$$\frac{\text{Number of CMDB entries recorded in the period}}{\text{Total number of CMDB records}} * 100$$

Frequency

    Measured: Monthly

    Reported: Monthly

Acceptable quality level: N/A

    Range: N/A

Set baseline of the percentage of recorded CMDB entries; measure and perform trend analysis over time. Expectation for this metric would be a sustained to upward trend from the baseline as the organization continues to grow and service offerings evolve.

Metric name

Percentage of accurately registered CIs in CMDB

Metric category

Service asset and configuration management

Suggested metric owner

Configuration manager

Typical stakeholders

IT operations manager, change manager, configuration manager, service level manager, service desk

Description

This metric shows the percentage of CIs that have been registered accurately in the CMDB. Depending on the level of confidence in the accuracy of CMDB entries, a KPI can be determined by checking a sample set of CIs.

Although many CIs are recorded using discovery and configuration tools, there are still several other CI types, such as documentation and services that require manual recording and can be prone to errors.

Measurement description

Formula:

$$\frac{\text{Number of accurately registered CIs in the CMDB}}{\text{Total number of CIs in the CMDB}} * 100$$

Frequency

    Measured: Monthly

    Reported: Monthly

Acceptable quality level: 95%

    Range: < 95% unacceptable (service asset management possibly out of control)

                     = 95% acceptable (maintain/improve)

                     > 95% exceeds (indicates service assets are well managed)

Note

This AQL allows up to 5% inaccurate service asset CI record entries to account for CMDB update lag time (i.e. time between change approval and CMDB entry) and data entry errors.

Release and deployment management metrics

Metrics applied to Release and deployment management (RDM) provide the necessary insight to process performance. The metrics in this section are linked to KPIs identified for activities in undertaken in this process. The metrics presented in this section are:

- Percentage of releases deployed without prior testing
- Percentage of releases without approved fallback plans
- Number of RFCs raised during Early Life Support (ELS) for a new or changed service
- Percentage of releases deployed with known errors
- Number of scheduled new or changed service releases pending.

Metric name

Percentage of releases deployed without prior testing

Metric category

Release and deployment management

Suggested metric owner

Deployment manager

Typical stakeholders

IT operations manager, information security manager, service desk, configuration manager

Description

This is a measure for assessing the effectiveness of release/release package planning and implementation management. This metric also provides an indicator of deployment risk exposure (i.e. lower percentage = lower risk).

Measurement description

Formula:

$$\frac{\text{Number of releases deployed without verification testing}}{\text{Total number of releases deployed}} * 100$$

Frequency

    Measured: Monthly

    Reported: Monthly

Acceptable quality level: All releases should be tested

    Range: < 99% of the time unacceptable (improvement opportunity)

    = 99% of the time acceptable (maintain/improve)

    > 99% of the time exceeds (process maturity level 4 or 5 potential)

Note

Meeting the AQL target 99% of the time allows for emergency changes as one per cent of the deployed releases.

Metric name

Percentage of releases without approved fallback plans

Metric category

Release and deployment management

Suggested metric owner

Release manager

Typical stakeholders

IT operations manager, information security manager, service desk, configuration manager

Description

This is a measure for assessing the effectiveness of release/release package planning and implementation management. This metric also provides an indicator of service continuity risk exposure (i.e. lower percentage = lower risk).

Measurement description

Formula:

$$\frac{\text{Number of releases without an approved fallback plan}}{\text{Total number of releases deployed}} * 100$$

Frequency

Measured: Monthly

Reported: Monthly

Acceptable quality level: 0%

Range: < 0% of the time unacceptable (improvement opportunity)

= 0% of the time acceptable (maintain/improve)

Note

Meeting the AQL target of 0% of the releases deployed with an approved Fallback Plan minimizes the release and deployment management cost, schedule and quality risk exposure.

Metric name

Number of RFCs raised during Early Life Support (ELS) for a new or changed service

Metric category

Release and Deployment Management (RDM)

Suggested metric owner

Release manager

Typical stakeholders

IT operations manager, information security manager, service desk, configuration manager

Description

This is a measure for assessing the effectiveness of release evaluation and validation testing. It can also be an indicator of deployed release/release package maturity. This metric is a simple tally of the number of RFCs for a new or changed service release within the defined post-deployment early life support period (e.g. two months) after implementation acceptance.

Measurement description

Formula: N/A

Change management tools offer an abundance of fields to collect change source information. It is recommended that the CMDB records include a field (e.g. a flag or comments) to reflect changes made during ELS. This measurement can be reported during the post-deployment review.

Frequency

    Measured: Monthly

    Reported: Monthly

Acceptable quality level: 0

    Range: N/A

Note

This measurement can provide inputs for trend analysis to evaluate the overall effectiveness of RDM efforts, including the quality of release/release package design and validation testing. It can also be useful as an indicator of potential RDM CSI opportunities.

Metric name

Percentage of releases deployed with known errors

Metric category

Release and deployment management

Suggested metric owner

Deployment manager

Typical stakeholders

IT operations manager, problem manager, service level manager, service desk, configuration manager

Description

This is a metric for monitoring the magnitude of unresolved problems/issues associated with the release of new or changed services. The measurement can also provide an indicator of release/release package quality, post-deployment problem management workloads and change management priorities. There are a number of issues that can cause these known errors, for instance:

- Unrealistic business expectations and requirements
- Design errors
- Vendor products
- Improper/inadequate testing
- Human error.

Measurement description

Formula:

$$\frac{\text{Number of releases deployed with known errors}}{\text{Total number of releases deployed}} * 100$$

Frequency

Measured: Monthly

Reported: Monthly

Acceptable quality level: 0%

> **Range:** < 95% unacceptable (improvement opportunity)
>
> = 95% acceptable (maintain/improve)
>
> > 95% exceeds (process maturity level 4 or 5 potential)

Note

The 95% AQL target allows for known errors associated with such actions as emergency change releases and/or source controlled CIs as five per cent of the releases.

Metric name

Number of scheduled new or changed service releases pending

Metric category

Release and deployment management

Suggested metric owner

Release manager

Typical stakeholders

IT operations manager, information security manager, service desk, configuration manager

Description

This is a measure of the queue for approved releases/ release packages. It can also provide an indicator of release and deployment management workloads and change management priorities in the ensuing period(s).

Measurement description

Formula: N/A

Simply the number of approved releases / release packages pending deployment in the change schedule.

Frequency

    Measured: Monthly

    Reported: Monthly

Acceptable quality level: 0

    Range: N/A

Service validation and testing metrics

Quality Assurance (QA) is the basis for Service Validation and Testing (SVT) efforts. The SVT process activities provide the mechanisms for assuring that released services (new or changed) meet performance objectives to deliver the intended utility (fitness for purpose) and warranty (fitness for use). The metrics presented in this section are:

- Percentage of risks with quantified risk assessment
- Percentage of risk register entries with a 'high' risk score
- Expected Monetary Value (EMV) of identified service risks
- Number of variances from service acceptance criteria
- Service test schedule variance
- Percentage of reusable test procedures
- Percentage of errors detected from pre-deployment testing
- Percentage of errors detected from testing in early life support.

Metric name

Percentage of risks with quantified risk assessment

Metric category

Service validation and testing

Suggested metric owner

Risk manager

Typical stakeholders

IT operations manager, service level manager, service desk, configuration manager

Description

This is a measure of the service risks that have been assessed with the quantified probability of risk event occurrence and the probable impact severity identified in the risk register. Service risks are assessed to determine criteria for validation and testing as part of minimizing service risk exposure. The metric is applied for evaluating performance of the risk management function.

Measurement description

Formula:

$$\frac{\text{Number of risks quantitatively assessed}}{\text{Total number of service risks identified}} * 100$$

Frequency

> **Measured:** Monthly
>
> **Reported:** Monthly

Acceptable quality level: 0%

> **Range:** > 0% unacceptable (service risks possibly out of control)
>
> = 0% of requirements acceptable (risk management function being properly performed)

Metric name

Percentage of risk register entries with a 'high' risk score

Metric category

Service validation and testing

Suggested metric owner

Risk manager

Typical stakeholders

IT operations manager, service level manager, service desk, configuration manager

Description

This is an overall measure of risk management effectiveness to minimize risk exposure as part of service design, transition and operation. It provides an overall service risk profile and can be applied for validating the service strategy as well as for identifying service improvement opportunities.

Measurement description

Formula:

$$\frac{\text{Number of identified risks with a high risk score}}{\text{Total number of risk register entries}} * 100$$

Frequency

> **Measured:** Monthly
>
> **Reported:** Monthly

Acceptable quality level: 10%

> **Range:** > 10% unacceptable (service risks possibly out of control)
>
> = 10% acceptable (maintain/improve)
>
> < 10% exceeds (indicates well-managed service risks)

Metric name

EMV of identified service risks

Metric category

Service validation and testing

Suggested metric owner

Risk manager

Typical stakeholders

IT operations manager, service level manager, configuration manager

Description

This is a measure of the amount of Management Reserve (MR) that should be allocated for 'unknowns' in the delivery of a service. MR is the budget amount reserved for responding to risk events (i.e. unknowns). MR is derived from the sum of estimated financial cost impacts from risk events identified in the risk register. The MR is total estimated financial cost impact (EMV) that could be incurred if all identified service risk events actually occur.

This metric is useful for determining the value proposition for SVT activities. It is expressed as a percentage of the total service budget. The valuation diminishes as the service life cycle progresses through operational ELS and as service operations risk exposure declines over time.

Measurement description

Formula:

$$\frac{\text{Total expected monetary value of all identified service risks}}{\text{Total budget allocated for service delivery}} * 100$$

Frequency

> **Measured:** Monthly
>
> **Reported:** Quarterly

Acceptable quality level: 5%

> **Range:** > 5% unacceptable (service risks possibly out of control)
>
> = 5% acceptable (maintain/improve)
>
> < 5% exceeds (indicates well-planned and implemented services)

Metric name

Number of variances from service acceptance criteria

Metric category

Service validation and testing

Suggested metric owner

Change manager

Typical stakeholders

IT operations manager, information security manager, service level manager, service desk, configuration manager

Description

This is a measure of the tested performance differences (variances) of new or changed services as compared to the approved service acceptance criteria. Variances may be identified by such evidence as test errors, configuration audit results and unresolved known errors. Understanding these variances provides the opportunity to accept or reject the variance prior to continuing to the next activity. These activities will be based on the decision to accept or reject.

Measurement description

Formula: N/A

It is simply reported as the number of variances from the customer-agreed acceptance criteria.

Frequency

> **Measured:** Monthly
>
> **Reported:** Monthly

Acceptable quality level: 0

> **Range:** N/A

Note

Variances from the acceptance criteria include, but are not limited to unfulfilled technical/functional performance, cost, schedule, and/or quality parameters. The metric should include any variance(s) for which a formal deviation or waiver has been approved.

Metric name

Service test schedule variance

Metric category

Service validation and testing

Suggested metric owner

Release manager

Typical stakeholders

IT operations manager, information security manager, service level manager, service desk, configuration manager

Description

This metric provides an understanding of the relationship between the approved (planned) and incurred (actual) schedule for service testing. Calculated in either labor hours or calendar days, planned versus actual test schedule performance is measured for any test activities during the development, release and deployment, and early life support of new and changed services.

Measurement description

Formula:

$$\frac{\text{Approved test schedule}-\text{actual test schedule}}{\text{Approved test schedule}} * 100$$

Note

Positive value is favorable (Ahead of schedule)

Negative value is unfavorable (Behind schedule)

Frequency

>**Measured:** Monthly
>
>**Reported:** Monthly

Acceptable quality level: +/- 5% Variance from the approved test schedule

>**Range:** > 5% variance unacceptable (test schedule possibly out of control)
>
>= 95% to 105% acceptable (maintain/improve)
>
>< 5% variance exceeds (indicates well-managed test activities)

Metric name

Percentage of reusable test procedures

Metric category

Service validation and testing

Suggested metric owner

Release manager

Typical stakeholders

IT operations manager, information security manager, service level manager, configuration manager

Description

This measurement identifies the quantity of reusable test procedures and associated test scripts (or use cases) as a ratio compared to all approved test procedures in a testing database or repository. Reusable test procedures can be identified in the repository (i.e. flagged) as having been used for the testing of more than one new or changed service release. These procedures should be considered as CIs therefore, the testing repository should be part of the CMS.

This metric provide indications of testing program effectiveness, service warranty and the alignment of services to the business.

Measurement description

Formula:

$$\frac{\text{Number of reusable test procedures}}{\text{Total number of approved test procedures}} * 100$$

Frequency

> **Measured:** Monthly
>
> **Reported:** Quarterly

Acceptable quality level: N/A

> **Range:** N/A

Set baseline percentage of reusable test procedures in the CMDB; measure and perform trend analysis over time. Expectation for this metric would be a sustained to upward trend from the baseline.

Metric name

Percentage of errors detected from pre-deployment testing

Metric category

Service validation and testing

Suggested metric owner

Release manager

Typical stakeholders

IT operations manager, service desk, configuration manager

Description

This measurement identifies the errors detected from testing prior to deployment, as compared to total errors detected from testing the service in all stages. It is useful as an indicator of pre-deployment testing effectiveness and provides insight to potential SVT improvement opportunities. Comprehensive testing and detection of most/all service errors prior to deployment is a significant part of minimizing service deployment costs and schedules.

Measurement description

Formula:

$$\frac{\text{Number of errors detected from pre-deployment testing}}{\text{Total number of errors detected from testing of a service}} * 100$$

Frequency

> **Measured:** Monthly
>
> **Reported:** Monthly

Acceptable quality level: 95%

> **Range:** < 95% unacceptable (improvement opportunity)
>
> = 95% acceptable (maintain/improve)
>
> > 95% exceeds (process maturity level 4 or 5 potential)

Metric name

Percentage of errors detected from testing in early life support

Metric category

Service validation and testing

Suggested metric owner

Change manager

Typical stakeholders

IT operations manager, customer, service desk, configuration manager

Description

This measurement identifies the errors detected from testing during ELS, as compared to total errors detected from testing the service in all stages. It is useful as an indicator of initial service quality and provides insight to potential SVT improvement opportunities. Service errors incurred during ELS can increase service deployment costs and acceptance schedules.

Errors detected during ELS provide customers/users with indicators of potential service performance issues and can negatively influence customer satisfaction. Accordingly, the SVT process emphasizes pre-deployment detection and resolution of errors.

Measurement description

Formula:

$$\frac{\text{Number of errors detected from early life support testing}}{\text{Total number of errors detected from testing of a service}} * 100$$

Frequency

Measured: Monthly

Reported: Monthly

Acceptable quality level: 5%

Range: > 5% unacceptable (improvement opportunity)

= 5% acceptable (maintain/improve)

< 5% exceeds (process maturity level 4 or 5 potential)

Change evaluation metrics

The purpose of Change Evaluation (EVA) is to provide consistent and standardized means for predictive assessment of service change impacts on the business. This is a decision support process invoked by the Change Advisor Board (CAB) to determine the actual performance of a service change as compared to its predicted performance. The metrics provided in this section are:

- Percentage of RFCs Evaluated
- Number of scheduled change evaluations pending
- Number of evaluated changes with variances from service acceptance criteria
- Percentage of RFCs rejected after EVA
- Customer satisfaction
- Quality defects identified from EVA.

Metric name

Percentage of RFCs evaluated

Metric category

Change evaluation

Suggested metric owner

Change manager

Typical stakeholders

IT operations manager, service level manager, configuration manager

Description

This is a measure of the number of requested changes for which a detailed EVA was performed — as a percentage of all RFCs. The metric is valuable as an indicator of the overall complexity of RFCs (evaluations are typically invoked for more complex changes).

It can also be useful as an input to assessing service risk exposure from RFCs. In general the probabilities of unforeseen negative impacts from implementing changes are inversely proportional to the percentage of RFCs evaluated. Accordingly, this metric also provides a high-level input for determining the EVA process value proposition.

Measurement description

Formula:

$$\frac{\text{Number of RFCs subjected to EVA}}{\text{Total number of RFCs}} * 100$$

Frequency

> **Measured:**   Monthly
>
> **Reported:**   Monthly

Acceptable quality level: N/A — baseline and trend

> **Range:**   N/A

Set EVA percentage baseline; measure and perform trend analysis over time. The expectation for this metric would be an upward trend from the baseline.

Metric name

Number of scheduled EVAs pending

Metric category

Change evaluation

Suggested metric owner

Change manager

Typical stakeholders

IT operations manager, information security manager, service desk, configuration manager

Description

This is a measure of the RFCs queue for new and changed services pending EVA. It provides an indicator of the change management workload and priorities in the ensuing period(s).

Measurement description

Formula: N/A

Simply report the number of RFCs pending EVA in the forward schedule of changes.

Frequency

    Measured: Monthly

    Reported: Monthly

Acceptable quality level: 0

    Range: N/A

Metric name

Number of evaluated changes with variances from service acceptance criteria

Metric category

Change evaluation

Suggested metric owner

Change manager

Typical stakeholders

IT operations manager, information security manager, service level manager, service desk, configuration manager

Description

This is a measurement of the performance differences (variances) of evaluated changed services for which EVAs were conducted as compared to the approved service acceptance criteria. Variances may be identified by such evidence as test errors, configuration audit results and unresolved known errors.

This metric is closely linked to the 'Number of variances from service acceptance criteria' metric in *Service validation and testing*. The distinctive attribute of this metric is that it considers changed services that were subjected to EVA.

Measurement description

Formula: N/A

It is simply reported as the number of changes implemented after EVA for which there were variances from the customer-agreed acceptance criteria.

Frequency

> **Measured:**   Monthly
>
> **Reported:**   Monthly

Acceptable quality level: 0

> **Range:**   N/A

Note

Variances from the acceptance criteria include, but are not limited to unfulfilled technical/functional performance, cost, schedule, and/or quality parameters. The metric should include any variance(s) for which a formal deviation or waiver has been approved.

Metric name

Percentage of RFCs rejected after EVA

Metric category

Change evaluation

Suggested metric owner

Change manager

Typical stakeholders

IT operations manager, information security manager, configuration manager

Description

This is a measure for assessing the volume of RFC rejection based on EVA, as a percentage of the combined total of all RFCs for new and changed services. An important task of EVA is to provide recommendations to the change manager concerning the disposition of the change.

The metric provides analytical insight to the value of the EVA process in its contribution to change management decision making.

Measurement description

Formula:

$$\frac{\text{RFCs rejected after EVA}}{\text{Total number of RFCs}} * 100$$

Frequency

> **Measured:** Monthly

> **Reported:** Quarterly

Acceptable quality level: N/A

> **Range:** N/A

Set baseline percentage of disapproved RFCs; measure and perform trend analysis over time. Expectation for this metric would be a downward trend from the baseline.

Metric name
Customer satisfaction

Metric category
Change evaluation

Suggested metric owner
Change manager

Typical stakeholders
IT operations manager, service level manager

Description
This is a measure of customer satisfaction with service changes, based on responses to customer satisfaction surveys, on a five-point scale. Measuring customer satisfaction with delivered services is an ongoing activity that gives service providers vital feedback in the form of a performance score.

Measurement description
Formula: N/A, see range

Frequency

> **Measured:** Monthly
>
> **Reported:** Monthly

Acceptable quality level: 3

> **Range:**
>
> > 1 = Not satisfied
> >
> > 2 = Slightly dissatisfied
> >
> > 3 = Generally satisfied/not dissatisfied
> >
> > 4 = Very satisfied
> >
> > 5 = Exceeds expectations

Metric name

Quality defects identified from EVA

Metric category

Change evaluation

Suggested metric owner

Change manager

Typical stakeholders

IT operations manager, information security manager, configuration manager

Description

This is a measure of the number of quality defects identified through the EVA process. Following service validation and testing, EVA will review and report the test results to change management. This report should include recommendations for improving the change and any other inputs to expedite decisions within change management.

This metric provides a Quality Control (QC) figure of merit for the EVA process.

Measurement description

Formula: N/A

It is simply the number of qualitative defects identified in evaluated change releases/release packages based on established workmanship standards and customer-agreed service acceptance criteria.

Frequency

> **Measured:** Monthly
>
> **Reported:** Monthly

Acceptable quality level: 0

> **Range:** N/A

Set baseline number of defects per work product; measure and perform trend analysis over time. Expectation for this metric would be a downward trend from the baseline.

Knowledge management metrics

In simplest terms, knowledge management is the translation of tacit knowledge to explicit knowledge. The Knowledge Management (KNM) process is applied to provide a shared knowledge base of service-related data and information available to stakeholders. An SKMS provides the central, controlled access repository of service information. The metrics in this section are:

- Percentage of formally assessed ITSM processes
- Percentage of contracts with remaining terms of 12 months or less
- Percentage growth of the SKMS
- Number of searches of the SKMS
- Percentage growth of SKMS utilization
- Number of SKMS audits (within a defined period).

Metric name

Percentage of formally assessed ITSM processes

Metric category

Knowledge management

Suggested metric owner

Service manager

Typical stakeholders

IT operations manager, service level manager, customers

Description

A formal ITSM process assessment provides a benchmark of the assessed process maturity level, by each process attribute, as well as identifying opportunities for process and service improvements.

This assessment can be performed by an internal team which may provide a bias toward the process or be limited by the knowledge of the assessment team. Assessments can also be performed by an external team offering industry experience and knowledge for a well-rounded assessment however, this will increase costs.

Measurement description
Formula:

$$\frac{\text{Number of formally assessed ITSM processes}}{\text{Total number of implemented ITSM processes}} * 100$$

Frequency
Measured: Quarterly

Reported: Annually

Acceptable quality level: N/A
Range: N/A

Set the baseline percentage of formally assessed ITSM processes; measure and perform trend analysis over time. Expectation for this metric would be a sustained to upward trend from the baseline.

Metric name
Percentage of service contracts with remaining terms of 12 months or less

Metric category
Knowledge management/supplier management

Suggested metric owner
Contract manager

Typical stakeholders
IT operations manager, service level manager, customer relationship manager, business relationship manager

Description

Monitoring and reporting on service contracts that have less than one year remaining on the contract terms provides timely reviews, renegotiation or termination of those contracts. This metric provides insight into the rate of service contract turnover and helps in business forecasting.

The 12-month time horizon can be adjusted to match patterns of business activity. A key element of this metric is to provide the service provider adequate time to prepare for service contract renewals, consider service retirements, revise associated supplier contracts and/or organizational level agreements (OLAs), and assess the change schedule.

Measurement description

Formula:

$$\frac{\text{Number of contracts with less than 12 months remaining}}{\text{Total number of existing service contracts}} * 100$$

Frequency

Measured: Monthly

Reported: Monthly

Acceptable quality level: N/A

Range: N/A

Set baseline for the percentage of contracts with remaining terms of 12 months or less; measure and perform trend analysis over time. Expectation for this metric would be a sustained trend from the baseline depending on the level of contract turnover and sustainment.

Metric name

Percentage growth of the SKMS

Metric category

Knowledge management

Suggested metric owner

Knowledge manager

Typical stakeholders

Process managers, management, service desk, suppliers

Description

As additional information is collected and store within controlled repositories, these repositories can be part of the SKMS or can be added to the SKMS based on the value provided to the organization. In either case they add to the collective knowledge of the organization and should be managed by KNM.

This metric can be measured in multiple ways when looking at SKMS growth. This first can be based on record counts while the second can measure the number of repositories within the SKMS.

Measurement description

Formula: The first is the record count metric.

$$\frac{\text{Number of SKMS records}}{\text{Previous number of SKMS records}} - 1 * 100$$

The second is measuring repository growth.

$$\frac{\text{Number of SKMS repositories}}{\text{Previous number of SKMS repositories}} - 1 * 100$$

This metric should be monitored and collected regularly to observe the SKMS growth from both the record and repository perspective. Both metrics combined provide a clear indication of overall SKMS growth.

Frequency

> **Measured:** Monthly

> **Reported:** Quarterly

Acceptable quality level: Baseline the initial metric and trend over time.

Range: N/A

Metric name

Number of searches of the SKMS

Metric category

Knowledge management

Suggested metric owner

Knowledge manager

Typical stakeholders

Process managers, management, service desk, suppliers

Description

The SKMS exists to provide organizational knowledge to all stakeholders. Therefore, the searches of the SKMS must be monitored to ensure not only its use to the organization but also to the value it provides in support of customers and services. The SKMS should be the first place everyone goes to for information.

This upward trending metric helps monitor the number of searches within the SKMS. As individuals learn to use it, the SKMS can provide valued information and their utilization will increase as the SKMS is seen as a trusted source of information and knowledge.

Measurement description

Formula: N/A

This metric can be collected from the tools used to manage the SKMS repositories. The level of monitoring may increase as more individuals require the needed information found within the SKMS. As this grows monitoring collection and reporting may increase as well.

Frequency

    Measured: Weekly/monthly

    Reported: Monthly/quarterly

Acceptable quality level: N/A

    Range: N/A

Metric name

Percentage growth of SKMS utilization

Metric category

Knowledge management

Suggested metric owner

Knowledge manager

Typical stakeholders

Process managers, management, service desk, suppliers

Description

As the SKMS matures and increases its value throughout the organization, the utilization should increase dramatically. SKMS utilization can include:

- Searches
- Adding new files (documentation)
- Updating information
- File reads.

This metric monitors the overall utilization within a defined period of time. The SKMS will be populated by several tools which may not be included in this metric as several records are added and updated daily.

Measurement description

Formula:

$$\frac{\text{Number of SKMS accesses}}{\text{Previous number of SKMS accesses}} - 1 * 100$$

As seen above, several activities can be included in the utilization. Therefore, prior to collecting this metric be sure to define the type of access that will be counted as utilization. The KNM tools and monitors will then help collect these metric data.

Frequency

Measured: Weekly

Reported: Monthly

Acceptable quality level: Baseline the initial metric and monitor trending patterns.

Range: Growth ranges can be set after a pattern of utilization is identified.

Metric name

Number of SKMS audits (within a defined period)

Metric category

Knowledge management

Suggested metric owner

Knowledge manager

Typical stakeholders

Process managers, management, service desk, suppliers

Description

The success of the SKMS relies in the organization's trust in the information and knowledge provided within the repositories. Therefore, regular audits of the SKMS must occur to ensure the highest level of quality of the information. The audit will include:

- Policy, process and procedures documentation
- File and records audit
- SKMS maintenance (change records)
- Utilization and performance reports
- Incidents and problems reported.

Audits should be performed by KNM for an overall service provider review. The organization should plan both internal and external audits from a business standpoint to maintain an unbiased perspective of the SKMS.

Measurement description

Formula: N/A

This metric should count all formal audits performed on the SKMS and the Knowledge Management process. It should distinguish between the types of audits performed and by whom.

Frequency

    Measured: Quarterly

    Reported: Annually

Acceptable quality level: N/A

    Range: N/A

CHAPTER 6: SERVICE OPERATION METRICS

Service operation is where the majority of metrics are collected as production services are provided to the customers. Service operation achieves effectiveness and efficiency in the delivery and support of services, ensuring value for both the customer and the service provider. Service operation maintains operational stability while allowing for changes in the design, scale, scope and service levels. This stage of the lifecycle is the culmination of the efforts provided in strategy, design, and transition. Service operation represents the successful efforts for the previous lifecycle phases to the customers with the successful delivery of services and creating high levels of customer satisfaction.

Operational metrics are used primarily in operations to maintain the infrastructure and within CSI to find opportunities for improvement. The metrics in this chapter are tied to the processes found in service operation. The metrics sections for this chapter are:

Event management metrics

Incident management metrics

Request fulfillment metrics

Problem management metrics

Access management metrics

Service desk metrics.

Event management metrics

This process is extremely important to just about all metrics. Monitoring the environment is a major aspect of event management and the pre-defined monitors will collect a majority of the measurements. These metrics are in line with several KPIs that support this process. The metrics presented in this section are:

- Percentage of events requiring human intervention
- Percentage of events that lead to incidents
- Percentage of events that lead to changes
- Percentage of events categorized as exceptions
- Percentage of events categorized as warnings
- Percentage of repeated events
- Percentage of events resolved with self-healing tools
- Percentage of events that are false positives
- Number of incidents resolved without business impact.

Metric name

Percentage of events requiring human intervention

Metric category

Event management

Suggested metric owner

Operations center management

Typical stakeholders

Technical staff, service desk, customer

Description

While event management relies upon tools for monitoring and managing events, there is still a need for staff to be involved to resolve and close certain events.

This downward trending metric provides an understanding of staff involvement with event management. It can also help determine if the organization is truly exploiting the full benefits of the tools used within event management. Increasing the number of events managed with the available tools will improve consistency and timeliness of event resolution and will allow staff to focus on more complex tasks.

Measurement description

Formula:

$$\frac{\text{Number of events requiring staff}}{\text{Total number of events}} * 100$$

This metric should be monitored regularly to ensure progress is made in the utilization of tools to resolve events. This will also demonstrate a more proactive approach to managing the environment.

Frequency

Measured: Monthly

Reported: Monthly

Acceptable quality level: 25%

Range: > 25% unacceptable (CSI opportunity)

= 25% acceptable (maintain/improve)

< 25% exceeds (Reset AQL to lower level)

Metric name

Percentage of events that lead to incidents

Metric category

Event management

Suggested metric owner

Operations center management

Typical stakeholders

Technical staff, service desk, customer, SLM

Description

As more of the environment is monitored, exceptions (those having significance to services) can be captured, categorized and escalated to the appropriate process in an expeditious manner. In particular, are those exceptions that require incident management processing.

This upward trending metric will assist in the speed in which incidents are resolved. While it would be optimum to reduce the number of incidents, the ability to capture them quickly, within event management, will reduce downtime and increase customer satisfaction.

Measurement description

Formula:

$$\frac{\text{Number of events as incidents}}{\text{Total number of events}} * 100$$

Utilizing this metric in combination with Incident Management metrics will provide a more complete picture of the life of an incident and how the organization is maturing in managing events and incidents.

Frequency

  Measured: Monthly

  Reported: Monthly

Acceptable quality level: N/A

  Range: N/A

Metric name

Percentage of events that lead to changes

Metric category

Event management

Suggested metric owner

Operations center management

Typical stakeholders

Technical staff, service desk, customer, change management, SLM

Description

There can be multiple reasons for an exception event to be handled by change management. These include:

- Threshold warnings
- Monitoring patch levels
- Configuration scans
- Software license monitoring.

Any of these situations may require an RFC in order to properly manage the necessary change to either establish or re-establish the norm or monitoring threshold. This demonstrates how event management creates a more proactive environment for managing services and increasing value to the customers.

Measurement description

Formula:

$$\frac{\text{Number of events as change}}{\text{Total number of events}} * 100$$

Utilizing this metric in combination with change management metrics will provide a more complete picture of the change and how the organization is maturing with event and change management.

Frequency
> **Measured:** Monthly
> **Reported:** Monthly

Acceptable quality level: N/A
> **Range:**   N/A

Metric name

Percentage of events categorized as exceptions

Metric category

Event management

Suggested metric owner

Operations center management

Typical stakeholders

Technical staff, service desk, customer

Description

Exception events are events that require additional handling and are past to other processes for further action. These processes are usually:

- Incident management
- Change management
- Problem management.

This metric provides a high level look at these types of events and, in particular, demonstrates the volume of exception events as compared to all events. This can be an important metric for an organization trying to become more proactive revealing measurable actions such as:

- Improved use of automation
- Expeditious handling of incidents
- Creating more standard/pre-approved changes
- Identification of potential problems.

Measurement description

Formula:

$$\frac{\text{Number of events as exceptions}}{\text{Total number of events}} * 100$$

The growth and maturation of event management will not only help identify these types of event but will ultimately help prevent or eliminate through process integration.

Frequency

    Measured: Monthly

    Reported: Quarterly

Acceptable quality level: N/A

    Range: N/A

Metric name

Percentage of events categorized as warnings

Metric category

Event management

Suggested metric owner

Operations center management

Typical stakeholders

Technical staff, service desk, customer

Description

As you can see from previous metrics, categorization of events is extremely important to determine how the event will be handled. For many organizations, the most common type of managed event will be warning events. These include:

- Threshold warnings
- Job scheduling
- System responses.

This upward trending metric allows the organization to become more proactive in service provision. A warning event allows actions to be taken to prevent an outage and becoming an exception event.

Measurement description

Formula:

$$\frac{\text{Number of events as warnings}}{\text{Total number of events}} * 100$$

The metric is usually based against thresholds set within capacity and availability management.

Frequency

> **Measured:** Monthly
>
> **Reported:** Quarterly

Acceptable quality level: N/A

> **Range:** N/A

Metric name

Percentage of repeated events

Metric category

Event management

Suggested metric owner

Operations center management

Typical stakeholders

Technical staff, service desk, customer

Description

This metric provides an understanding of the amount of repeated events, primarily those categorized as warnings or exceptions, which occur within the environment. Reoccurring events can be the most problematic for service delivery, while damaging the reputation of the organization. Once detected, these events can be forwarded to problem management for further actions and elimination.

As with many other event management metrics, this metric enhances the organization's ability to be more proactive in managing and providing services.

Measurement description

Formula:

$$\frac{\text{Number of repeated events}}{\text{Total number of events}} * 100$$

This measurement can be categorized in many ways to better understand the occurrences. Categorizations include:

- By occurrence type
- By service
- By overall events
- By CI
- By configuration category or CI type.

Frequency

     Measured: Monthly

     Reported: Quarterly

Acceptable quality level: N/A

     Range: N/A

Metric name

Percentage of events resolved with self-healing tools

Metric category

Event management

Suggested metric owner

Operations center management

Typical stakeholders

Technical staff, service desk, customer

Description

This metric provides an indication of the overall exploitation of tools and automation when handling events. Repeatability and consistency are found in using tools to provide corrective actions when events occur. Self-healing tools utilize scripts to analyze and correct certain types of events (usually simple corrective actions). Not all events can be handled by these types of tools. Careful consideration must be taken when selecting which events will be handled in this manner.

We suggest creating policies to provide direction in the use of self-healing tools and to enhance decision making within the event management process. This should be an upward trending metric as organizations become more familiar with events and the self-healing tools used to correct them.

Measurement description

Formula:

$$\frac{\text{Number of events resolved by tools}}{\text{Total number of events}} * 100$$

The metric may be provided within an ITSM tool or within the self-healing tools. In many cases, measurements from both tools will provide a comprehensive view of this metric.

Frequency

> **Measured:** Monthly
>
> **Reported:** Quarterly

Acceptable quality level: 10% (increase this percentage over time)

> **Range:** < 10% unacceptable (improvement opportunity)
>
> = 10% acceptable (maintain/improve)
>
> > 10% exceeds (continue exploring more uses)

Metric name

Percentage of events that are false positives

Metric category

Event management

Suggested metric owner

Operations center management

Typical stakeholders

Technical staff, service desk, customer

Description

False positive events are nuisances to the staff and waste valuable time trying to investigate and manage. This metric demonstrates improvement opportunities within the service or processes. It can help identify areas throughout the service management lifecycle that might have missed certain items or have not thought of these items.

Once a false positive is discovered, the monitoring tool can be corrected or that area of monitoring can be eliminated if deemed unnecessary.

Measurement description

Formula:

$$\frac{\text{Number of false positive events}}{\text{Total number of events}} * 100$$

You may experience difficulties finding tools to identify and report this type of metric. These types of events may need manual re-categorization while working within the event management process. If this metric is utilized, ensure the process has a procedure or work instructions to address these events.

Frequency

> **Measured:** Monthly
>
> **Reported:** Quarterly

Acceptable quality level: 1%

> **Range:** > 1% unacceptable (CSI opportunity)
>
> = 1% acceptable (maintain/improve)
>
> < 1% exceeds (best practice potential)

Metric name

Number of incidents resolved without business impact

Metric category

Event management and incident management

Suggested metric owner

Operations center management/incident manager

Typical stakeholders

Technical staff, service desk, customer, SLM

Description

While it seems focused on incident management, this metric could be a direct indication of the benefit event management provides. Proactively monitoring the environment to discover real time issues allows incident management to resolve the incident prior to impacting the business.

The relationship between incident and event management can have a dramatic impact to the way incidents are managed. As both processes continue to mature, a proactive nature within the organization will become the norm which will increase service provision and customer satisfaction.

Measurement description

Formula: N/A

An integrated service management tool or suite of tools can provide this metric. It may also require integration with monitoring tools.

Frequency

> **Measured:** Monthly
>
> **Reported:** Quarterly

Acceptable quality level: N/A

> **Range:** N/A

Incident management metrics

Incident management has been deemed the major process of service operation. This process is all about keeping services running and customers satisfied. Incident management is a reactive process however, if integrated with event management these reactive activities can have a proactive nature (what we call 'proactively reactive'). That is, reacting and resolving an incident before they impact the organization. These metrics are in line with several KPIs that support this process. The metrics presented in this section are:

- Average incident resolution time
- Average escalation response time
- Percentage of re-opened incidents
- Incident backlog
- Percentage of incorrectly assigned incidents
- First call resolution
- Percentage of re-categorized incidents.

Metric name

Average incident resolution time

Metric category

Incident management

Suggested metric owner

Incident manager

Typical stakeholders

Caller, service desk, required IT functions, service owner, SLM

Description

This metric represents the average time taken to resolve an incident to the customer's satisfaction. Average resolution time should be based on the assigned priority. An example is shown below:

- Priority 1 – 2 hrs
- Priority 2 – 4 hrs
- Priority 3 – 8 hrs
- Priority 4 – 24 hrs.

Resolution times must be negotiated and documented within the incident management process. Any service requiring different resolution time should be documented within the SLA.

Measurement description

Formula:

$$\frac{\text{Accumulated incident resolution time}}{\text{Total number of resolved incidents}}$$

This measurement should be gathered in pre-defined timeframes (e.g. daily or weekly). The metric can be calculated for all incidents or broken down by incident priority for a more detailed view. In addition, ITSM tools can provide the number of incidents that failed to meet the prioritized resolution time. This can be used to identify potential issues within the incident management process.

Frequency

Measured: Weekly

Reported: Monthly

Acceptable quality level: Meet each priority level, for example:

Range:

- Priority 1 – 2 hrs
- Priority 2 – 4 hrs
- Priority 3 – 8 hrs
- Priority 4 – 24 hrs.

Metric name

Average escalation response time

Metric category

Incident management

Suggested metric owner

Incident manager

Typical stakeholders

Caller, service desk, required IT functions, service owner, SLM

Description

This metric represents the average time taken for the initial response by a tier two or tier three team to an escalated incident. Average response time should be based on the assigned priority. For example:

- Priority 1 – 15 minutes
- Priority 2 – 30 minutes
- Priority 3 – 1 hrs
- Priority 4 – 2 hrs.

Response times must be negotiated and documented within the incident management process. Any service requiring different response times should be documented within the SLA.

Measurement description

Formula:

$$\frac{\text{Accumulated incident response time}}{\text{Total number of escalated incidents}}$$

This measurement should be gathered in pre-defined timeframes (e.g. weekly or monthly). The metric can be calculated for all escalated incidents or broken down by priority for a more detailed view of escalations. In addition, ITSM tools can provide the number of incidents that failed to meet the prioritized response time. This can be used to identify potential issues within the escalation procedure.

Frequency

> **Measured:** Weekly

> **Reported:**   Monthly

Acceptable quality level: Meet each priority level, for example:

> **Range:**

- Priority 1 – 15 minutes
- Priority 2 – 30 minutes
- Priority 3 – 1 hrs
- Priority 4 – 2 hrs.

Metric name

Percentage of re-opened incidents

Metric category

Incident management

Suggested metric owner

Incident manager

Typical stakeholders

Caller, service desk, required IT functions, service owner, SLM

Description

This metric represents the percentage of tickets re-opened due to occurrences such as:

- Inadequate resolution
- Dissatisfied customers
- Improper incident documentation
- Incident re-occurrence within a set period of time (24 hours).

This should be a low to downward trending metric. Re-opened tickets show a possible lack of due diligence within the incident management process as key activities could have been missed or improperly performed. A persistent percentage might demonstrate an opportunity for either process improvement(s) or additional training for incident management staff.

Measurement description

The number of re-opened tickets will be collected over a period of time within the ITSM tool and compared against the total number of closed tickets during that same timeframe.

Formula:

$$\frac{\text{Number of re-opened tickets}}{\text{Total number of closed tickets}} * 100$$

This measurement should be gathered in pre-defined timeframes (e.g. weekly or monthly). Some ITSM tools will not allow a closed incident to be re-opened, making this metric unobtainable. Therefore, other metrics can be used or created to better understand the occurrences described above.

Frequency

> **Measured:** Weekly
>
> **Reported:** Monthly

Acceptable quality level: 2%

> **Range:** > 3% unacceptable (CSI opportunity)
>
> = 2% acceptable (maintain/improve)
>
> < 2% exceeds (best practice potential)

Metric name
Incident backlog

Metric category
Incident management

Suggested metric owner
Incident manager

Typical stakeholders
Caller, service desk, service owner, SLM

Description
A backlog of any type can create issues for service provision. An incident backlog is compounded by the fact that service issues exist and customers may be directly affected by the incident which might impact the business. This metric can be used to demonstrate one or multiple issues including:

- Service desk capacity
- High average incident resolution time
- Incident storms
- ITSM tool issues
- Changes to services or processes.

Measurement description
Typically, this measurement is represented by the incident queue length found within the ITSM tool. Another measurement that becomes equally important is the queue time. These measurements can be viewed in real time or as an average within a defined period of time.

Formula:

$$\frac{\text{Total time of all incidents in queue}}{\text{Total number of incidents in queue}}$$

These measurements should be gathered in pre-defined timeframes (e.g. hourly or daily) and should be reported in increments such as hourly, by shift or within business critical timeframes.

Frequency

> **Measured:** Weekly

> **Reported:** Monthly

Acceptable quality level: Defined by business requirements and reported as averages within defined timeframes. These timeframes can be specified within an SLA.

> **Range:** Defined in the SLAs

Metric name

Percentage of incorrectly assigned incidents

Metric category

Incident management

Suggested metric owner

Incident manager

Typical stakeholders

Caller, service desk, required IT functions, service owner, SLM

Description

Assigning an incident is critical to the timely escalation and resolution of the issue. If not done properly, incorrectly assigned incidents can cause the ticket to bounce from one group to another while the caller(s) remain without a resolution, wasting time and resources.

This should be a low to downward trending metric. A cause for this issue can be found in the method of incident categorization either within the process or ITSM tool.

Utilization of incident models and templates can help to reduce this issue.

Measurement description

Incorrectly assigned incidents can be found in the number of re-assignments logged within the ITSM tool.

Formula:

$$\frac{\text{Number of re-assigned incidents}}{\text{Total number of closed incidents}} * 100$$

This measurement should be gathered within a defined timeframe (i.e. weekly, monthly). The results from this metric can provide insights into:

- Increased use to templates within the tool
- Better training for service desk agents
- Process improvements.

Frequency

Measured: Weekly

Reported: Monthly

Acceptable quality level: 10%

Range: > 10% unacceptable (CSI opportunity)

= 10% acceptable (maintain/improve)

< 10% exceeds (best practice potential)

Metric name

First call resolution

Metric category

Incident management

Suggested metric owner

Incident mana

Typical stakeholders

Caller, service desk, service owner, SLM

Description

The knowledge and expertise of the service desk are critical when executing incident management. This metric demonstrates the maturity of the service desk as more incidents should be resolved by the service desk without escalation.

Of course, all incidents cannot be resolved by the service desk due to complexity of the incident, security levels, authorization levels, or experience. However, as knowledge is gained, documented and shared, higher levels of first call resolution will become the norm for incident management while increasing the value of the service desk.

Measurement description

ITSM tools provide either a resolved by field or tab (some have both) to document the individual or team that resolved the incident. Searching and reporting on this field will provide the resolution source and demonstrate how the service desk is maturing.

Formula:

$$\frac{\text{Number of SD resolved incidents}}{\text{Total number of resolved incidents}} * 100$$

This measurement should be gathered incrementally in predefined timeframes (i.e. weekly, monthly). Further investigation into resolved incidents will show sources of knowledge used to resolve these incidents (i.e. known error database or KEDB).

Frequency

Measured: Weekly

Reported: Monthly

Acceptable quality level: Develop a baseline and trend going forward

Range: N/A

Metric name
Percentage of re-categorized incidents

Metric category
Incident management

Suggested metric owner
Incident manager

Typical stakeholders
Caller, service desk, service owner

Description
Proper categorization has a dramatic impact to the handling of all incidents. This can be seen during escalation and using/updating the CMS/CMDB.

This should be an upward trending metric. Re-categorizing an incident can occur during the lifecycle of the incident or in reviewing the incident after is has been resolved. No matter when this occurs, it is vital that the incident is properly categorized as it will become part of your knowledge base.

Measurement description
Many ITSM tools provide the ability to monitor and track changes to the incident categorization. Searching and reporting on this field(s) will provide valuable information on incident categorization, process efficiency, and will demonstrate how the service desk is maturing.

Formula:

$$\frac{\text{Number of re-categorized incidents}}{\text{Total number of resolved incidents}} * 100$$

This measurement should be gathered over a period of time (i.e. weekly, monthly). Further investigation into incident categorization will improve the handling of incidents and the information contained in the CMS/CMDB.

Frequency

    Measured: Weekly

    Reported: Monthly

Acceptable quality level: 10%

    Range: > 10% unacceptable (CSI opportunity)

                     = 10% acceptable (maintain/improve)

                     < 10% exceeds (best practice potential)

Request fulfillment metrics

Service requests require consistent handling and a centralized entry point for customers. Request fulfillment processes these service requests and with integration into the service catalog provides a standardized and consistent entry point from which customers can access and request services. These metrics are in line with several KPIs that support this process. The metrics presented in this section are:

- Percentage of overdue service requests
- Service request queue rate
- Percentage of escalated service requests
- Percentage of correctly assigned service requests
- Percentage of pre-approved service requests
- Percentage of automated service requests.

Metric name

Percentage of overdue service requests

Metric category

Request fulfillment

Suggested metric owner

Service desk manager

Typical stakeholders

End users, customers, service desk, SLM

Description

There is an expectation for delivery when providing requests to customers. Typically, service requests are made through the service catalog or directly to the service desk. In either case, it is appropriate to provide a delivery date or time for the request. The delivery date and time can be specified in the service catalog or an SLA.

Those requests that do not meet their specified delivery schedule are considered overdue and must be reported. This metric provides customers and management a view of how service requests are managed from a high level.

Measurement description
Formula:

$$\frac{\text{Number of overdue requests}}{\text{Total number of requests}} * 100$$

Requests, no matter how big or small, are important to the individual customers. If, for any reason, a request cannot be provided in a timely manner, communicate this to the customer prior to the delivery date/time. While the customer will not be pleased with the delay, they will appreciate the proactive communication.

Frequency
Measured: Monthly
Reported: Monthly
Acceptable quality level: 10%
Range: > 10% unacceptable (CSI opportunity)

= 10% acceptable (maintain/improve)

< 10% exceeds (best practice potential)

Metric name
Service request queue rate

Metric category
Request fulfillment

Suggested metric owner

Service desk manager

Typical stakeholders

End users, customers, service desk

Description

The request queue can back up quickly based on the number of requests, time of the year or any number of other situations which cause an increased need from customers and users.

A build-up of the request queue can be a result of several events including:

- New service demand
- Increase in customer/user base
- Major service change
- Request storms
- Security issues or changes.

Measurement description

This measurement is represented by the request queue length found within the ITSM tool. The request queue time is equally as important to understand the magnitude of the requests in queue. These metrics can be viewed in real time or as averages within a defined period of time.

Formula:

$$\frac{\text{Accumulated time of all requests in queue}}{\text{Total number of requests in queue}} * 100$$

These measurements should be gathered within a defined timeframe (i.e. hourly, daily) and should be reported in increments such as hourly or by shift. These can also be categorized by priority yielding greater meaning for the queue time.

Frequency

   Measured: Weekly

   Reported: Monthly

Acceptable quality level: Baseline and trend

   Range: N/A

Metric name

Percentage of escalated service requests

Metric category

Request fulfillment

Suggested metric owner

Service desk manager

Typical stakeholders

End users, customers, service desk

Description

This metric represents the percentage of service requests that are escalated to higher tier levels for resolution. While depending on the type of organization, this can be a downward trending metric as more requests are automated within the service catalog or resolved by the service desk.

The metric can help to demonstrate the maturity of the request fulfillment process. It will complement the amount of time required to resolve and close service requests.

Measurement description

Formula:

$$\frac{\text{Number of escalated requests}}{\text{Total number of requests}} * 100$$

This measurement should be gathered within a defined timeframe (i.e. weekly). It is recommended that this metric is reviewed on a monthly to quarterly basis.

Frequency

>**Measured:** Monthly
>
>**Reported:** Quarterly

Acceptable quality level: 25%

>**Range:**   > 25% unacceptable (CSI opportunity)
>
>   = 25% acceptable (maintain/improve)
>
>   < 25% exceeds (consider AQL reset)

Metric name

Percentage of correctly assigned service requests

Metric category

Request fulfillment

Suggested metric owner

Service desk manager

Typical stakeholders

End users, customers, service desk, tier level teams, SLM

Description

Service requests that require greater authority or functional knowledge and experience are escalated to higher tier teams and, therefore, should be assigned properly. This ensures the prompt handling of the request and increases closure time.

While many requests will follow a scripted path (i.e. programmed work flow), there are circumstances when human intervention is required, script errors occur, and/or *ad hoc* requests are made — all can cause assignment errors which delay the fulfillment of the request.

Measurement description

Formula:

$$\frac{\text{Number of requests not re-assigned}}{\text{Total number of requests}} * 100$$

This can be a difficult metric to capture depending on the ITSM tool and its attributes. Some tools can collect changed team assignments and report them as standard features of the tool. Others might not have this capability and might require methods such as log searches to determine if request assignments have been changed. Scripts can be created to help automate these types of searches and regularly scheduled based on reporting targets or requirements.

Frequency

    Measured: Weekly

    Reported: Monthly

Acceptable quality level: 98%

    Range: < 98% unacceptable (tool or process improvements)

                  = 98% acceptable (maintain/improve)

                  > 98% exceeded

Metric name

Percentage of pre-approved service requests

Metric category

Request fulfillment

Suggested metric owner

Service desk manager

Typical stakeholders

End users, customers, service desk, management

Description

This metric represents the percentage of service requests that have prior approval for processing and demonstrates efficiencies gained as requests are delivered to customers. Many requests (security, acquisition, general management) require authorization for fulfillment to the customer's satisfaction. Depending on the types of requests, such as above, some may not be pre-approved. Frequently submitted requests can be approved based on known low risk and thus expedited with an automated work flow model built into the ITSM tool.

Measurement description

Formula:

$$\frac{\text{Number of pre-approved requests}}{\text{Total number of requests}} * 100$$

Once a request is designated as pre-approved, consider creating a template or script within the ITSM tool automation to fulfill the request providing higher levels of consistency and performance. This will also allow greater accuracy in measuring the volume of requests and reporting findings.

Frequency

Measured: Monthly

Reported: Monthly

Acceptable quality level: 25% (look for opportunities to increase)

Range: < 25% unacceptable (process improvement opportunity)

= 25% acceptable (maintain/improve)

> 25% exceeds (reset objectives to higher level)

Metric name

Percentage of automated service requests

Metric category

Request fulfillment

Suggested metric owner

Service desk manager

Typical stakeholders

End users, customers, service desk

Description

Many ITSM tools provide methods to automate the handling of service requests to increase the speed and efficiency of fulfillment. Other requests may require manual intervention due to the nature of the request (security, high cost purchases, authorization level).

Careful consideration needs to be taken when considering automating a service request. We recommend creating a methodology to review the request and walk through all aspects of fulfilling the request. Once fully understood and approved, the request can be automated within a request model or template. This should be an upward trending metric as the process and understanding requests matures.

Measurement description

Formula:

$$\frac{\text{Number of automated requests}}{\text{Total number of requests}} * 100$$

This measurement can be directly related to an automated tool-based service catalog. Many service catalog tools have automated workflow capabilities which create consistent execution of the activities required to fulfill the request. Request categorization and request types can assist in determining which requests would be best served in an automated manner.

Frequency

> **Measured:** Monthly
>
> **Reported:** Monthly

Acceptable quality level: 25% (to start with but increased to an aggressive goal, such as 75%)

> **Range:** < 25% unacceptable (improvement opportunity)
>
> = 25% acceptable (maintain/improve)
>
> > 25% exceeds (grow/improve)

Problem management metrics

Problem management metrics should help mature process activities to help this process become proactive; resolving potential issues before they occur. Problem management records known errors and provides an incredible knowledge base to incident management in the form of the KEDB. These metrics are in line with several KPIs that support this process. The metrics presented in this section are:

- Problem management backlog
- Number of open problems
- Number of problems pending supplier action
- Number of problems closed in the last 30 days
- Number of known errors added to the KEDB
- Number of major problems opened in the last 30 days
- KEDB accuracy.

Metric name

Problem management backlog

Metric category

Problem management

Suggested metric owner

Problem manager

Typical stakeholders

Service desk, required IT functions, suppliers

Description

This metric represents the number of problems found within a problem queue that are creating a backlog. This backlog can be caused by a number reasons including:

- Supplier involvement

- Pending changes
- System or service complexity
- Customer involvement or approval.

The problem backlog can be managed within an ITSM tool and should be reviewed regularly by the problem manager and/or team. The backlog should be reported via time (i.e. months in the queue).

Measurement description

Formula: N/A

This measurement should be gathered within a defined timeframe (i.e. monthly, quarterly). This measurement is reported as the number of problems in the queue and the length of time (30, 60, 90 days) in the queue. This backlog must be managed as it can have a direct impact to incident and change management as well as many business processes.

Frequency

    Measured: Monthly

    Reported: Monthly, quarterly

Acceptable quality level: Minimum number determined by the organization

    Range: N/A

Metric name

Number of open problems

Metric category

Problem management

Suggested metric owner

Problem manager

Typical stakeholders

Service desk, required IT functions, suppliers, management

Description

This metric includes problems found in several states including:

- Open (working)
- Pending (on hold)
- In queue (backlogged).

Open problems provide opportunities to the organization. Many problems can be created in a more proactive manner allowing the organization to prevent problems from either occurring or re-occurring. All problems must be prioritized to ensure proper handling and to establish a level of importance to the organization.

A well-managed number of problems are a sign of a healthy organization in that it can demonstrate both the reactive nature of problems (working in conjunction with incident management) or being more proactive (linking to availability management) and trying to be opportunistic.

Measurement description

Formula: N/A

This measurement can be easily found in most ITSM tools. If this is not possible, a manual search of problems with active state (as seen above) can provide this measurement.

Frequency

Measured: Monthly

Reported: Monthly

Acceptable quality level: Minimum number determined by the organization

Range: N/A

Metric name

Number of problems pending supplier action

Metric category

Problem management

Suggested metric owner

Problem manager

Typical stakeholders

Service desk, required IT functions, suppliers, supplier management, SLM

Description

Many problems can be created due to supplier issues or known problems. When this occurs the resolution of the problem is out of the hands of problem management and becomes dependent on the supplier.

Resolution for the problem could be found in:

- An existing patch (quick fix)
- A custom-built patch
- Within the next release of patches
- Within the next release of the component (i.e. OS, application, drivers, etc.).

If this is the case, beware of any service level targets for problem management as you no longer have control which could result in a breached target.

Measurement description

Formula: N/A

There is no measurement for this metric but should still be managed at as low a level as possible. This number should be gathered within a defined timeframe (i.e. monthly). This type of problem can be categorized within the ITSM tool providing a simple manner to collect and extract this metric.

Frequency

> **Measured:**   Monthly
>
> **Reported:**   Monthly

Acceptable quality level: N/A

> **Range:**   N/A

Metric name

Number of problems closed in the last 30 days

Metric category

Problem management

Suggested metric owner

Problem manager

Typical stakeholders

Service desk, SLM

Description

This metric is important to determine the progress and maturity of problem management. Once the problem resolution is implemented and accepted in production, formal closure of the problem must occur as documented in the process documentation. When the problem is opened the problem ticket becomes part of the knowledge base for future reference.

The time period and its starting point must be defined (e.g. weekly, monthly, quarterly) to create consistency for this metric.

This metric can be used to measure problem closures in longer terms such as 60, 90 and 120-day increments. The timeframe(s) should be based on organizational needs.

Measurement description

Formula: N/A

This should be an upward trending metric compared to the number of tickets opened. The upward trend will demonstrate improvements in problem management and problem solving techniques. This metric should be gathered within a defined timeframe such as those described in the description.

Frequency

> **Measured:**   Dependent upon the time period defined

> **Reported:**   Dependent upon the time period defined

Acceptable quality level: N/A

> **Range:**   N/A

Metric name

Number of known errors added to the KEDB

Metric category

Problem management

Suggested metric owner

Problem manager

Typical stakeholders

Service desk, knowledge management, suppliers, technical teams

Description

This metric observes activities pertaining to the Known Error Database (KEDB). While problem management will continue to create known errors due to existing problems, proactive problem management will research and find potential problems and create known errors prior to the occurrence of an incident.

The KEDB is a valuable tool for incident management and should be kept up to date and protected at all times. This is one of the first repositories searched when trying to resolve an incident.

Measurement description

Formula: N/A

This should be an upward trending metric particularly when proactive problem management techniques are being used. Known errors related to a problem should have a status assignation based on the current status of the problem. This will keep the KEDB relevant to current issues within the organization.

Frequency

> **Measured:** Monthly
>
> **Reported:** Quarterly

Acceptable quality level: N/A

> **Range:** N/A

Metric name

Number of major problems opened in the last 30 days

Metric category

Problem management

Suggested metric owner

Problem manager

Typical stakeholders

Service desk, technical team, suppliers, management, SLM

Description

Major problems are described as those that are extreme or even catastrophic to the organization and may require additional authority or resources to minimize impact.

Therefore, the hope is that major problems are kept to a minimum.

While this metric is concerned with the number of major problems opened within a defined period, it is equally important to measure major problems closed and reviewed. This will help ensure the all major problems are properly managed.

Measurement description

Formula: N/A

The optimum number would be zero as no organization wants to experience problems at this level. However, since 'stuff happens' we must proactively manage our environments to avoid and/or minimize these types of problems. This measurement should be gathered within a defined timeframe (i.e. monthly).

Frequency

> **Measured:** Monthly
>
> **Reported:** Monthly, quarterly, annually (as required)

Acceptable quality level: N/A

> **Range:** N/A

Metric name

KEDB accuracy

Metric category

Problem management

Suggested metric owner

Problem manager

Typical stakeholders

Service desk, knowledge management, suppliers, technical teams

Description

As mentioned in a previous metric, the KEDB is a valuable tool for incident management and is used continuously as incidents are captured and diagnosed. This creates a dependency on the accuracy of the information provided as the incidents occur in real time and have priority levels which set resolution targets. Poor KEDB information can delay resolution and breach SLA targets.

The information within the KEDB must be regularly monitored for accuracy through:

- Examination of incidents
- Routine audits of the KEDB
- Technical reviews of the root cause and workaround.

Measurement description

Formula:

$$\frac{\text{Number of KEs found in error}}{\text{Total number of KEs}} * 100$$

In addition, ITSM tools can provide incident and problem information on the creation and use of the KEDB.

Frequency

Measured: Monthly

Reported: Quarterly

Acceptable quality level: 100% Accuracy

Range: < 100% unacceptable (audit and correct)

= 100% acceptable

Access management metrics

This process is closely related to information security management. Security management creates security policies dealing with all aspects of security. Access management executes activities that are in line and support those policies. These metrics are in line with several KPIs that support this process. The metrics presented in this section are:

- Percentage of invalid user IDs
- Percentage of requests that are password resets
- Percentage of incidents related to access issues
- Percentage of users with incorrect access.

Metric name

Percentage of invalid user IDs

Metric category

Access management

Suggested metric owner

Security manager (i.e. CISO)

Typical stakeholders

Security, service desk, management, audit

Description

The unfortunate truth is that many organizations do not properly manage user IDs. As people move on, either within the organization or externally, there are instances where user IDs are not removed and remain on the network.

This metric provides an understanding of the amount of IDs that have no ownership (staff assigned) and are considered invalid. This can occur from situations such as:

- Transfers and promotions
- Termination (usually voluntary)
- Change in employee status (family leave)
- Multiple user IDs for individuals
- Managing vendors or contractors.

In many cases invalid user IDs are not found and reported until a security audit is performed (either internal or external).

Measurement description

Formula:

$$\frac{\text{Number of invalid user IDs}}{\text{Total number of user IDs}} * 100$$

This metric should be monitored regularly to ensure the overall protection of the organization and the assets used to provide service.

Frequency

> **Measured:** Monthly
>
> **Reported:** Monthly

Acceptable quality level: 0% (more of a goal)

> **Range:** N/A

Metric name

Percentage of requests that are password resets

Metric category

Access management

Suggested metric owner

Security manager (i.e. CISO)

Typical stakeholders

Security, service desk, management, request fulfillment, customers

Description

The intricacies and complexity of password standards can lead to a high volume of password resets. Password standards should be based on a security policy as well as the management of passwords.

This metric will show the volume of password resets and can provide insight into potential problems with password standards. The metric can also demonstrate a need for automation of password resets (i.e. self-help tools).

Measurement description

Formula:

$$\frac{\text{Number of password reset requests}}{\text{Total number of service requests}} * 100$$

This metric will depend on how the organization performs password resets. If resets are performed via a service request the formula above can be used. However, if a self-help tool is used, measurements and metrics from the tool can be used to understand password resets.

Frequency

Measured: Monthly

Reported: Monthly

Acceptable quality level: N/A

Range: N/A

Metric name

Percentage of incidents related to access issues

Metric category

Access management

Suggested metric owner

Security manager (i.e. CISO)

Typical stakeholders

Security, service desk, incident management

Description

Security-related incidents are initially handled by the service desk, however there may be separate security procedures to authorize resolution of access-related incidents by other groups. Sensitivity to access issues may be greater with organizations with classified systems and services. Access incidents may include:

- Insufficient access rights granted
- Improper level of access granted
- Exposure to sensitive information (e.g. intellectual property)
- Security breach
- Unprotected assets.

Careful consideration and additional training are necessary when developing procedures to handle access related incidents. Information security management must be consulted when developing or changing these procedures.

Measurement description

Formula:

$$\frac{\text{Number of access related incidents}}{\text{Total number of incidents}} * 100$$

Ensure proper identification and categorization of these incidents prior to incident closure. Reporting frequency will depend upon the type of organization and level of security for systems and services.

Frequency

> **Measured:** Daily or weekly
>
> **Reported:** Weekly or Monthly

Acceptable quality level: < 1%

> **Range:** ≥ 1% unacceptable
>
> < 1% acceptable
>
> 0% exceeds

Metric name

Percentage of users with incorrect access

Metric category

Access management

Suggested metric owner

Security manager (i.e. CISO)

Typical stakeholders

Security, service desk, management, event management, customers

Description

This metric can be used to understand the amount of users with improper rights. This can include:

* Insufficient access
* Inappropriate access rights
* Incorrect group access.

Proper access requires the appropriate level of authorization from management. While access is granted via management approval, in many cases incorrect access is not found until one of these events occur:

- User requests a change or corrections in access
- An access related incident occurs
- An external or internal security audit
- A security clean-up gets underway.

Measurement description
Formula:

$$\frac{\text{Number of users with incorrect access}}{\text{Total number of users}} * 100$$

Collection of the number of users with incorrect access may come from multiple sources such as event management, incident management and request fulfillment.

Frequency

    Measured: Weekly

    Reported: Monthly

Acceptable quality level: < 1%

    Range: > 1% unacceptable

                 < 1% acceptable

                 0% exceeds

Service desk metrics

The service desk is a function within service operations. Many of the operational processes are carried out by the service desk. Therefore, the service desk should be considered as a vital function for all organizations. These metrics are in line with several KPIs that support this function. The metrics presented in this section are:

- Average call duration
- Average number of calls per period
- Number of abandoned calls
- Average customer survey results
- Average call hold time.

Metric name

Average call duration

Metric category

Event management

Suggested metric owner

Operations center management

Typical stakeholders

Service desk, customers, incident management, SLM

Description

This metric is directly measuring the customer's experience with the service desk. We must understand that the customer's experience begins with the call initiation not when a call is answered. Therefore call duration should include:

- Voice Response Unit (VRU) time
- Active call time
- Voice survey time

- Queue time
- Hold time.

Consistent management of this metric will:
- Help increase customer satisfaction
- Assist in reducing costs
- Improve management of resources
- Reduce call duration.

Measurement description
Formula:

$$\frac{\text{Total accumulated call time for all calls}}{\text{Total number of number of calls}}$$

Utilizing this metric in combination with incident management or request fulfillment metrics will provide a more complete picture of the customer's experience with the service desk.

Frequency

    Measured: Weekly

    Reported: Monthly

Acceptable quality level: Established by management

    Range: Based on established AQL

Metric name
Average number of calls per period

Metric category
Service desk

Suggested metric owner
Service desk manager

Typical stakeholders

Service desk, customers, management

Description

One of the first things required for this metric is to have the period clearly defined. This metric will then help understand the volume of calls within the defined period.

This metric is useful for planning the total staffing of the service desk as well as the staffing requirements within the defined periods. Industry statistics are available to help plan resources based on call volumes, however, understanding these statistics only provides guidance for staffing levels. Industry formulas are also available to improve staffing decisions.

Measurement description

Formula:

$$\frac{\text{Total accumulative calls for a number of periods}}{\text{Total number of periods}}$$

For this metric, define the number of periods to use for the collection of information and measurements (e.g. five periods, Monday – Friday for a business week). Collecting all calls during those five periods will then provide the information required to calculate this metric.

Frequency

      Measured: Weekly

      Reported: Monthly

Acceptable quality level: N/A

      Range: N/A

Metric name

Number of abandoned calls

Metric category

Service desk

Suggested metric owner

Service desk manager

Typical stakeholders

Service desk, customers

Description

Abandoned calls create a direct customer perception of poor service. This metric represents the number of abandoned calls within a defined period of time (i.e. daily, weekly). Abandoned calls are calls which the customer disconnected prior to receiving service. The usual issue behind abandoned calls is the wait time within the queue.

This metric should be viewed regularly by the service desk and managed to the lowest possible number.

Measurement description

Formula:

This measurement can be collected from the Automated Call Distribution (ACD) function of the telephony system. The metric should be presented as a number rather than a percentage as high call volumes can make a percentage seem relatively low. If a percentage is required please reference the formula below.

$$\frac{\text{Total number of abandoned calls in a period}}{\text{Total number of calls in a period}} * 100$$

Combined with other metrics such as, average number of calls per period, the service desk manager can better manage staff and resource levels to meet customer needs.

Frequency

> **Measured:** Weekly
>
> **Reported:** Monthly

Acceptable quality level: Determine current baseline

> **Range:** Strive to continually lower the baseline

Metric name

Average customer survey results

Metric category

Service desk

Suggested metric owner

Service desk manager

Typical stakeholders

Service desk, management, customers

Description

This metric provides an understanding of the customer's experience with the service desk and satisfaction level. Appropriate satisfaction levels and definition must be discussed and agreed upon by management prior to the release of any survey.

As the organization's surveys mature, utilize metrics from other processes to increase the understanding of survey results. This will help increase the organization's knowledge as to why the results are at their current levels.

Measurement description

Formula:

$$\frac{\text{Total accumulated survey scores}}{\text{Total number of surveys returned}}$$

Survey scores must be translated into management information. The scores should be categorized into meaningful information such as:

- Outstanding
- Highly satisfied
- Satisfied
- Dissatisfied
- Very dissatisfied.

At times, numbers don't have the meaning or impact necessary so we recommend using wording.

Frequency

    Measured: Monthly

    Reported: Quarterly

Acceptable quality level: Highly satisfied

    Range: Based on categorization

Metric name

Average call hold time

Metric category

Service desk

Suggested metric owner

Service desk management

Typical stakeholders

Service desk, customer

Description

This metric can be gathered from the ACD function of a telephony system. This is an extremely important metric as it represents the customer's experience when calling the service desk.

This metric can help determine potential resource issues on the service desk. When discussing hold times, use your own experience as a customer to fully understand how to manage calls. Managing the length of hold times will have a dramatic impact on improved customer satisfaction ratings. Do not underestimate managing this metric.

Measurement description
Formula:

$$\frac{\text{Total accumulated hold time}}{\text{Total number of calls on hold}}$$

In many cases, this metric will be a standard within the ACD function. If not, the measurements can usually be easily extracted and calculated via an external tool such as a spreadsheet.

Frequency

    Measured: Monthly

    Reported: Quarterly

Acceptable quality level: Defined by the organization

    Range: Set and maintain as low a hold time as possible

CHAPTER 7: ADDITIONAL METRICS

A wide range of operational infrastructure systems, resources, capabilities, and processes may be part of IT service delivery. The focus of this chapter is the processes, outside of the service management lifecycle, that support the business and the service provider. The information in this chapter provides metrics for those additional processes that support the provision of services. The metrics sections for this chapter are:

Project management metrics

Risk management metrics

Data center metrics.

Project management metrics

Metrics most commonly applied in project management are based on Earned Value Management (EVM) for monitoring and controlling cost and schedule performance. These are standard measurements that provide the means of objectively determining variances from planned performance, evaluating the root causes, and gauging corrective actions.

Other important service performance measurements used for managing service projects (quality, risk, etc.) are provided throughout the book in sections that address specific service lifecycle processes. The metrics in this section are:

- Cost Variance (CV)
- Cost Variance Percentage (CV %)
- Cost Performance Index (CPI)
- Cost Estimate at Completion (Cost EAC)
- Estimate To Complete (ETC)
- Percent Complete (% Complete)
- Percent Spent (% Spent)

- Schedule Variance (SV)
- Schedule Variance Percentage (SV %)
- Schedule Performance Index (SPI)
- Schedule Estimate at Completion (Schedule EAC).

Metric name

Cost Variance (CV)

Metric category

Program/project management

Suggested metric owner

Program/project manager

Typical stakeholders

IT operations manager, service manager

Description

This is the standard measurement for cost performance as measured by comparing the budgeted value of work accomplished with the actual costs incurred for accomplishing that work.

Measurement description

Formula:

Budgeted cost of work performed − Actual cost of work performed

Note

The CV is a value reported conventionally in monetary terms but can be stated in labor hours or other units of production. It is also expressed as a percentage derived from comparison to the approved Performance Measurement Baseline (PMB).

Frequency

The CV is calculated for each period (i.e. monthly) and cumulatively applying the accrued (i.e. to date) BCWP and ACWP values.

> **Measured:** Monthly
>
> **Reported:** Monthly

Acceptable quality level: +/- 10% Variance from the approved PMB

> **Range:** > +/- 10% unacceptable (project costs possibly out of control)
>
> = 90% to 110% of budgeted costs acceptable (maintain/improve)
>
> < +/- 10% exceeds (indicates project costs are under control)

Metric name

Cost Variance Percentage (CV %)

Metric category

Program/project management

Suggested metric owner

Program/project manager

Typical stakeholders

IT operations manager, service manager

Description

This is the cost performance measurement yielded by the ratio of CV to EV. The metric is CV as a percentage of the overall budget performance to date. The BCWP or EV value applied can be monetary and/or labor hours as a commonly used valuation that reflects the approved budget.

Measurement description

Formula:

$$\frac{\text{Cost variance}}{\text{Budgeted cost of work performed}} * 100$$

Frequency

CV % is reported monthly across all project lifecycle phases to provide insight to the magnitude of periodic and cumulative budget risk exposure.

> **Measured:** Monthly
>
> **Reported:** Monthly

Acceptable quality level: +/- 10% of budgeted costs

> **Range:** > +/- 10% unacceptable (project costs possibly out of control)
>
> = 90% to 110% of budgeted costs acceptable (maintain/improve)
>
> < +/- 10% exceeds (indicates project costs are under control)

Metric name

Cost Performance Index (CPI)

Metric category

Program/project management

Suggested metric owner

Program/project manager

Typical stakeholders

IT operations manager, service manager

Description

This is a measurement of cost performance efficiency for work accomplished; expressed by the ratio of the budgeted value of work accomplished to actual costs incurred.

Measurement description

Formula:

$$\frac{\text{Budgeted cost of work performed}}{\text{Actual cost of work performed}}$$

Frequency

Measured: Monthly

Reported: Monthly

Acceptable quality level: +/- 0.10

Range: > +/- 0.10 unacceptable (project costs possibly out of control)

= 0.90 to 1.10 acceptable (maintain/improve)

< +/- 0.10 exceeds (indicates project costs are under control)

Metric name

Cost Estimate At Completion (Cost EAC)

Metric category

Program/project management

Suggested metric owner

Program/project manager

Typical stakeholders

IT operations manager, service manager

Description

This measurement is an empirically-based forecast of total costs that will be expended upon completion of a task, control account, or program/project. A conventional Cost EAC calculation is the BAC divided by the cumulative cost performance efficiency as shown by the Cost Performance Index (CPI).

Measurement description

Formula:

$$\frac{\text{Budget at completion}}{\text{Cost performance index}} * 100$$

Note

Initially (i.e. for planning) the Cost EAC is simply the sum of cost estimates for budget formation.

Frequency

Measured: Monthly

Reported: Monthly

Acceptable quality level: +/- 10% of BAC

Range: > +/- 10% unacceptable (project costs possibly out of control)

= 90% to 110% acceptable (maintain/improve)

< +/- 10% exceeds (indicates project costs are under control)

Metric name

Estimate To Complete (ETC)

Metric category

Program/project management

Suggested metric owner

Program/project manager

Typical stakeholders

IT operations manager, service manager

Description

This measurement is a forecast of the costs that will be incurred for remaining work based on the current level of cost performance efficiency. The ETC calculation considers the cumulative actual costs incurred to date in order to reflect only the value of remaining work as a component of the EAC.

Measurement description

Formula:

$$\frac{\text{Estimate at completion}}{\text{Budget at completion}} * 100$$

Note: Initially (i.e. during program/project planning) EAC = ETC = BAC, which is the sum of cost estimates for budget formation.

Frequency

Measured: Monthly

Reported: Monthly

Acceptable quality level: +/- 10% variance from BAC

Range:　　　> +/- 10% unacceptable (project costs possibly out of control)

= 90% to 110% acceptable (maintain/improve)

< +/- 10% exceeds (indicates project costs are under control)

Metric name

Percent Complete (% Complete)

Metric category

Program/project management

Suggested metric owner

Program/project manager

Typical stakeholders

IT operations manager, service manager

Description

This metric is a measurement of performance progress to date expressed by the ratio of the budget for work accomplished to the total authorized budget for all of the planned work.

Measurement description

Formula:

$$\frac{\text{Budgeted cost of work performed}}{\text{Budget at completion}} * 100$$

Note

Combined with the Percent Spent (% Spent) this metric provides a means of quickly evaluating the performance status.

Frequency

Measured: Monthly

Reported: Monthly

Acceptable quality level: The % Complete should be in line with the cumulative program/project costs.

Range: N/A

Metric name

Percent Spent (% Spent)

Metric category

Program/project management

Suggested metric owner

Program/project manager

Typical stakeholders

IT operations manager, service manager

Description

This metric is a measurement of budget expenditures to date expressed by the ratio of the actual costs incurred for work accomplished to the total authorized budget for all of the planned work.

Measurement description

Formula:

$$\frac{\text{Actual cost of work performed}}{\text{Budget at completion}} * 100$$

Note

Combined with the % Complete this metric provides a means of quickly evaluating the performance status.

Frequency

Measured: Monthly

Reported: Monthly

Acceptable quality level: The % Spent should be in line with the program/project performance schedule.

Range: N/A

Metric name

Schedule Variance (SV)

Metric category

Program/project management

Suggested metric owner

Program/project manager

Typical stakeholders

IT operations manager, service manager

Description

This is the standard measurement for schedule performance as measured by comparing the budgeted value of work accomplished with the budgeted costs of the work planned for completion in the period.

Measurement description

Formula:

> Budgeted cost of work performed − Budgeted cost of work scheduled

Note

The SV value is reported conventionally in monetary terms, but can be stated in labor hours or other units of production. It is also expressed as a percentage derived from comparison to the approved Performance Measurement Baseline (PMB).

Frequency

The SV is calculated for each period (i.e. monthly) and cumulatively applying the accrued (i.e. to date) BCWP and BCWS values.

Measured: Monthly

Reported: Monthly

Acceptable quality level: +/- 10% variance from the approved PMB

Range: > +/- 10% unacceptable (project schedule possibly out of control)

= 90% to 110% of scheduled costs acceptable (maintain/improve)

< +/- 10% exceeds (indicates project schedule is under control)

Metric name

Schedule Variance Percentage (SV %)

Metric category

Program/project management

Suggested metric owner

Program/project manager

Typical stakeholders

IT operations manager, service manager

Description

This is the schedule performance measurement yielded by the ratio of the Schedule Variance (SV) to the Planned Value (PV). The metric is SV as a percentage of the value of work scheduled to date. The BCWS or PV value applied can be monetary and/or labor hours as commonly used valuation that reflects the scheduled work.

Measurement description

Formula:

$$\frac{\text{Schedule variance}}{\text{Budgeted cost of work scheduled}} * 100$$

Frequency

SV % is reported monthly across all project lifecycle phases to provide insight to the magnitude of periodic and cumulative schedule risk exposure.

> **Measured:** Monthly
>
> **Reported:** Monthly

Acceptable quality level: +/- 10% of budgeted for scheduled work

> **Range:** > +/- 10% unacceptable (project schedule possibly out of control)
>
> = 90% to 110% of planned costs acceptable (maintain/improve)
>
> < +/- 10% exceeds (indicates project schedule is under control)

Metric name

Schedule Performance Index (SPI)

Metric category

Program/project management

Suggested metric owner

Program/project manager

Typical stakeholders

IT operations manager, service manager

Description

This is a measurement of schedule performance efficiency for work accomplished, expressed by the ratio of the budgeted value of work performed to budgeted value of work scheduled (i.e. planned).

Measurement description

Formula:

$$\frac{\text{Budgeted cost of work performed}}{\text{Budgeted cost of work scheduled}}$$

Frequency

> **Measured:** Monthly
>
> **Reported:** Monthly

Acceptable quality level: +/- 0.10

> **Range:** > +/- 0.10 unacceptable (project schedule possibly out of control)
>
> = 0.90 to 1.10 acceptable (maintain/improve)
>
> < +/- 0.10 exceeds (indicates project schedule is under control)

Metric name

Schedule Estimate At Completion (Schedule EAC)

Metric category

Program/project management

Suggested metric owner

Program/project manager

Typical stakeholders

IT operations manager, service manager

Description

This measurement is an empirically based forecast of the schedule at completion of a task, control account, or program/project. A conventional Schedule EAC calculation is the BAC divided by the cumulative schedule performance efficiency as shown by the SPI.

Measurement description

Formula:

$$\frac{\text{Budgeted at completion}}{\text{Schedule performance index}}$$

Note

Initially (i.e. for planning) the Schedule EAC is simply the sum of cost estimates for planned work applied in budget formation.

Frequency

>**Measured:** Monthly
>
>**Reported:** Monthly

Acceptable quality level: +/- 10% of BAC

>**Range:** > +/- 10% unacceptable (project schedule possibly out of control)
>
>= 90% to 110% acceptable (maintain/improve)
>
>< +/- 10% exceeds (indicates project schedule is under control)

Risk management metrics

The risk management process includes risk management planning, risk identification, risk analysis, risk response planning and risk monitoring and control. The overall objectives of risk management activities are to increase the probability and impact of positive events, and minimize the probability and impact of negative events.

Risk management focuses on the uncertainty of future events or conditions that will impact service performance objectives if they occur. The purpose of the risk management process is to monitor risk event indicators (the risk horizon) and be prepared to respond. The metrics in this section are:

- Average time to conduct a risk assessment
- Number of risk assessments performed (in a defined period)
- Number of outstanding remediation actions
- Number of active risks identified
- Number of closed risks (in a defined period).

Metric name

Average time to conduct a risk assessment

Metric category

Risk management

Suggested metric owner

Risk manager

Typical stakeholders

Customers, management, financial management, IT staff, suppliers, process owners

Description

A risk assessment evaluates the situation at hand and determines the probability of occurrence and the potential impact of risk. Assessments will require different timeframes and resources to fully evaluate all potential risks based on each situation.

This metric will define the average time required to conduct a risk assessment which will help to better plan the time needed for each assessment. Several organizations who find themselves in volatile industries have dedicated risk management departments. Depending on the size of the organization and the industry, a risk management department could become stretched to the resource limit very quickly and therefore, must plan appropriately.

Measurement description

Formula:

$$\frac{\text{Accumulated time for all assessments}}{\text{Total number of assessments}}$$

As mentioned above, this is a valuable planning metric for risk assessments. This metric can be categorized by the different types of assessments performed to improve the overall planning.

Frequency

> **Measured:** Quarterly
>
> **Reported:** Annually

Acceptable quality level: Create a baseline and monitor

> **Range:** Dependent on opportunities found for future services

Note

Average time should include assessment preparation time, the time for the assessment, and time after the assessment to analyze and create the risk report.

Metric name

Number of risk assessments performed (in a defined period)

Metric category

Risk management

Suggested metric owner

Risk manager

Typical stakeholders

Customers, management, financial management, IT staff, suppliers, process owners

Description

This metric is a simple counter for the number of risk assessments performed within a defined time period (i.e. annual, semi-annual). This metric can be used to justify resources, planning budgets, or for scheduling.

A risk assessment should be considered for all significant changes within the organization. For an IT service provider a risk assessment should occur for the following situations:

- New services added
- Major changes
- Facility changed
- Additional customers
- Mergers and acquisitions
- Adding or changing technology.

Measurement description

Formula: N/A

Understanding how many assessments are performed demonstrates the organization's commitment to risk management and prevention. The information gained from each assessment creates an accumulative knowledge that can be applied across the organization.

Frequency
>   **Measured:**   Quarterly
>   **Reported:**   Annually

Acceptable quality level: N/A
>   **Range:**   N/A

Metric name

Number of outstanding remediation actions

Metric category

Risk management

Suggested metric owner

Risk manager

Typical stakeholders

Customers, management, financial management, IT staff, suppliers, process owners

Description

Remediation action follows the risk assessment and is used to mitigate the findings of the assessment. These actions are created to respond to the findings and eliminate the threat of the risk. From the Management of Risk® (M_o_R®), the actions are categorized as:

- Transfer (move the risk to another party)
- Tolerate (accept and do nothing)
- Terminate (re-scope to remove)
- Treat (take actions to handle the risk).

This metric ensures the remediation actions are monitored and handled promptly. This metric can be enhance with associated information from the assessment such as the risk, risk priority, assessment, and associated change record.

Measurement description

Formula: N/A

The metric can be collected from a risk register or risk log. Change management reports can add value through the documented change record associated with the risk. The change report provides evidence of the remediation efforts and the success of the actions.

Frequency

    Measured: Quarterly

    Reported: Annually

Acceptable quality level: N/A

    Range: N/A

Metric name

Number of active risks identified

Metric category

Risk management

Suggested metric owner

Risk manager

Typical stakeholders

Customers, management, financial management, IT staff, suppliers, process owners

Description

Once identified, risks should be documented in a risk register or risk log and monitored regularly. Many risks can be mitigated quickly while others may require ongoing attention and monitoring. In either case, these active risks should be assigned to a risk owner and managed to protect the organization from the threat posed by the risk. Active risks can include:

- New risks from an assessment
- Risks being remediated
- Ongoing risks that are tolerated and monitored.

This metric provides an understanding of the risks that posed an active threat to services provided to the customer. Active risks should be prioritized based on the level and extent of the finding from the risk assessment.

Measurement description

Formula: N/A

A status field should be included within the risk register or risk log that will provide the current status, such as active, of the risk. This field can be used to report and manage the current risks to the organization.

Frequency

> **Measured:** Quarterly
>
> **Reported:** Annually

Acceptable quality level: N/A

> **Range:** N/A

Metric name

Number of closed risks (in a defined period)

Metric category

Risk management

Suggested metric owner

Risk manager

Typical stakeholders

Customers, management, financial management, IT staff, suppliers, process owners

Description

Closed risks provide a history of risk management actions and activities. These risks contain valuable knowledge of risks identified and managed which will help improve risk management going forward.

This metric demonstrates the ongoing activities of risk management and the success of mitigation action through closed risks. We recommend that all closed risks have the associated change record documented providing evidence for closure.

Measurement description

Formula: N/A

Input for this metric can be provided from multiple resources such as risk management, security, or auditing. It doesn't matter where the risk is identified as long as it is documented and managed properly.

Frequency

>   **Measured:**   Quarterly

>   **Reported:**   Quarterly

Acceptable quality level: N/A

>   **Range:**   N/A

Data center metrics

A data center is an IT services production and support environment, hosting the infrastructure required to provide services to the business. This section provides some basic measurements for evaluating and managing the data center environment.

It is important to note that this section is not intended as a data center engineering knowledge base. Rather, it provides some of the fundamental measurements that apply to the operation of data center environmental systems. The metrics presented are:

- Data center heating and cooling
- Data center primary power
- Data center backup power.

Metric name

Data center heating and cooling

Metric category

Data center environmental systems

Suggested metric owner

Facilities manager

Typical stakeholders

IT operations manager, service desk, change manager, process owners

Description

Heating, ventilation and air conditioning (HVAC) systems provide data center environmental temperature and humidity control. Heat transfers from hot to cold – 'cold' is created by removing heat and 'hot' is created by adding heat. Accordingly, the fundamental concept of data center

HVAC operations in a data center is the evacuation of heat from the environment.

British Thermal Units (BTUs) are commonly used as the measurement of heat. A BTU is the amount of heat required to raise the temperature of one pound (0.454 kg) of liquid water (0.1198 US gallons or 0.1 UK gallon) by 1°F (0.556°C). For cooling, a commonly used term is 'tons of cooling' which means an air conditioner can remove 12,000 BTUs of heat per hour (e.g. a 5 ton air conditioner removes 60,000 BTUs of heat per hour). For heating, the commonly used term is BTU/h (BTUs per hour) or MBH (1,000 BTUs per hour, where 'M' is the Roman numeral for 1,000).

These values are important for a fundamental understanding of heating and cooling systems that provide the data center operating environment for IT service assets.

Measurement description

Formulas:

- 1 BTU = 0.293071 Wh (*Watt hours*) (approximately)
- 1 Watt (1 W) = 3.41214 BTU/h (approximately)
- 1,000 BTU/h = 293.071 W (approximately)
- 12,000 BTU/h (in the US) = 3.51 kW of energy (approximately)

Frequency

    Measured: Monitored continuously for operations, assessed incrementally to determine the impact of the heat load from IT systems

    Reported: As required

Acceptable quality level: Establish the operational baseline, monitor and control in accordance with stipulated IT systems environmental operating parameters

    Range: N/A

Metric name

Data center primary power

Metric category

Data center electrical service

Suggested metric owner

Facilities manager

Typical stakeholders

IT operations manager, service desk, change manager, process owners

Description

IT systems require a constant supply of electricity for the sustained reliable operations to meet service availability targets. The electrical power loads of IT systems are expressed as either Watts or Volt-Amps (VA). The Watts rating is the real power drawn by the equipment. The VA rating is called the 'apparent power'" and is the product of the voltage applied to the equipment, times the current drawn by the equipment. The VA rating is always equal to or larger than the Watt rating. The ratio of the Watt to VA rating is the Power Factor (PF) and is expressed as a decimal number (e.g. 0.6) or a percentage (e.g. 60%).

The sum of the all data center equipment (IT systems and infrastructure systems) power ratings is used to determine the primary electrical capacity requirements. Generally, three-phase electrical service is standard for commercial facilities and single-phase electrical service is standard for residential facilities.

Measurement description

Formulas:

Electrical calculations	Volts x Amps = Watts or VA Volts = Watts / Amps Amps = Watts / Volts KVA (kilovolt-amps) = Volts x Amps / 1000 KW (kilowatts) = KVA x PF Watts = VA x PF Amps = (VA x PF) / Volts Volts = (VA x PF) / Amps
Single-phase electrical service	Watts = Volts x Amps
Three-phase electrical service	Watts = Volts x Amps x 1.73

Frequency

Measured: Incrementally as part of determining the impact of the power budget required for IT systems.

Reported: As required

Acceptable quality level: Establish the operational baseline, monitor and control within the primary electrical power available

Range: N/A

Metric name

Data center backup power

Metric category

Data center electrical service

Suggested metric owner

Facilities manager

Typical stakeholders

IT operations manager, service desk, change manager, process owners

Description

Backup power for IT systems are in the form of an uninterruptible power supply (UPS — also termed battery backup or static UPS) and backup generators (also termed emergency generators or rotary UPS). Battery UPS units are intended for short-term primary power loss (e.g. 15 minutes or less), while generators are for sustaining operations for long-term power outages. The sizing of these backup power sources is critical for ensuring data center COOP and the availability of services supported by the data center.

UPS systems may have both Watt ratings and VA ratings. It is an industry standard that the Watt rating is approximately 60% of the VA rating, as the typical power factor of common loads. Therefore, it is safe to assume that the Watt rating of the UPS is 60% of the published VA rating. The conservative UPS sizing approach is to ensure the sum of the equipment load ratings (Watts) is below 60% of the UPS VA rating. This usually results in an oversized UPS, thus a longer run time than expected.

Backup generators are typically rated in kilowatts (kW) with factory testing at a stipulated PF (e.g. 0.8 PF). Accordingly, either the Watts or VA load values can be used for sizing a generator. As for UPS units, the conservative approach is to use a standard or factory PF (e.g. 0.6 to 0.8) to the total VA load.

Measurement description

Formula:

Calculating the load for UPS and backup generator sizing	$Watts = VA \times PF$ $VA = Watts / PF$ $PF = Watts / VA$

Frequency

> **Measured:** Incrementally as part of determining the impact of the power budget required for IT systems

> **Reported:** As required

Acceptable quality level: Establish the operational baseline, monitor and control within the primary electrical power available

> **Range:** N/A

REFERENCES

Office of Government Commerce (2011), "ITIL® Service Strategy," The Stationery Office (TSO), London, England

Office of Government Commerce (2011), "ITIL® Service Design," The Stationery Office (TSO), London, England

Office of Government Commerce (2011), "ITIL® Service Transition," The Stationery Office (TSO), London, England

Office of Government Commerce (2011), "ITIL® Service Operation," The Stationery Office (TSO), London, England

Office of Government Commerce (2011), "ITIL® Continual Service Improvement," The Stationery Office (TSO), London, England

John R. Hauser and Gerald M. Katz (1998), "Metrics: You Are What You Measure," Working Paper, International Center for Research on the Management of Technology, MIT, Cambridge, MA 02142

Jane Chittenden (Lead) 2006, *Risk Management Based on M_O_R® A Management Guide*, Van Haren Publishing

Peter Brooks, Jan van Bon, and Tieneke (Editors) 2006, *Metrics for IT Service Management*, Van Haren Publishing, ITSMF

U.S. Department of Commerce National Institute of Standards and Technology, NIST Special Publication 800-53 "Recommended Security Controls for Federal Information Systems and Organizations," Revision 3, 2009; Priority 1 Controls CM-1, CM-2 (2, 4, 5), CM-3, CM-5 (2, 7), CM-7 (1, 2), CM-8 (1, 2, 3, 4, 6), CM-9, PM-6, SA-6, SA-7, RA-3 (a, b, c, d), RA-5 (a, b, 1, 2, 5, 6), SC-18, SC-26, SI-3 (a, b, 1, 2, 5, 6)

Ted Gaughan, PMP and Toby Gouker, Ph.D., *Control Account Manager's Handbook – An Earned Value Management Best Practice Reference*, Fifth Edition 2010, PA&E Global, Mount Airy, MD.

References

How to Convert VA to Watts and KVA to Kilowatts (2011), Retrieved from http://www.powerstream.com/VA-Watts.htm

A Guide to the Project Management Body of Knowledge (PMBOK®), Fourth Edition, ANSI/PMI 99-001-2008, Project Management Institute, Newton Square, PA, 2008.

Electronic Industries Alliance Standard "EIA-748-A Earned Value Management Systems." ANSI/EIA-748-A-1998, Approved: May 19, 1998 (Reaffirmed: August 28, 2002), Government Electronics and Information Technology Association Sector of the Electronic Industries Alliance, Arlington, VA, 1998.

ITG RESOURCES

IT Governance Ltd. sources, creates and delivers products and services to meet the real-world, evolving IT governance needs of today's organizations, directors, managers and practitioners.

The ITG website (*www.itgovernance.co.uk*) is the international one-stop-shop for corporate and IT governance information, advice, guidance, books, tools, training and consultancy.

http://www.itgovernance.co.uk/itsm.aspx is the information page on our website for IT service management resources.

Other Websites

Books and tools published by IT Governance Publishing (ITGP) are available from all business booksellers and are also immediately available from the following websites:

www.itgovernance.co.uk/catalog/355 provides information and online purchasing facilities for every currently available book published by ITGP.

http://www.itgovernance.eu is our euro-denominated website which ships from Benelux and has a growing range of books in European languages other than English.

www.itgovernanceusa.com is a US$-based website that delivers the full range of IT Governance products to North America, and ships from within the continental US.

www.itgovernanceasia.com provides a selected range of ITGP products specifically for customers in South Asia.

www.27001.com is the IT Governance Ltd. website that deals specifically with information security management, and ships from within the continental US.

Pocket Guides

For full details of the entire range of pocket guides, simply follow the links at *www.itgovernance.co.uk/publishing.aspx*.

Toolkits

ITG's unique range of toolkits includes the IT Governance Framework Toolkit, which contains all the tools and guidance that you will need in order to develop and implement an appropriate IT governance framework for your organization. Full details can be found at *www.itgovernance.co.uk/products/519*.

For a free paper on how to use the proprietary Calder-Moir IT Governance Framework, and for a free trial version of the toolkit, see *www.itgovernance.co.uk/calder_moir.aspx*.

There is also a wide range of toolkits to simplify implementation of management systems, such as an ISO/IEC 27001 ISMS or a BS25999 BCMS, and these can all be viewed and purchased online at: *http://www.itgovernance.co.uk/catalog/1*.

Best Practice Reports

ITG's range of Best Practice Reports is now at *www.itgovernance.co.uk/best-practice-reports.aspx*. These offer you essential, pertinent, expertly researched information on a number of key issues including Web 2.0 and Green IT.

Training Services

IT Governance offers an extensive portfolio of training courses designed to educate information security, IT governance, risk management and compliance professionals. Our classroom and online training programme will help you develop the skills required to deliver best practice and compliance to your organisation. They will also enhance your career by providing you with industry-standard certifications and increased peer recognition. Our range of courses offers a structured learning path from foundation to advanced level in the key topics of information security, IT governance, business continuity and service management.

ISO/IEC 20000 is the first international standard for IT service management and has been developed to reflect the best practice guidance contained within the ITIL® framework. Our ISO20000 Foundation and Practitioner training courses are designed to provide delegates with a compressive introduction and guide to the implementation of an ISO20000 management system and an industry-recognised qualification awarded by APMG International.

Full details of all IT Governance training courses can be found at *http://www.itgovernance.co.uk/training.aspx*.

Professional Services and Consultancy

As IT service management becomes ever more important in organisations, so the deployment of best practice (e.g. ITIL®), or the development of a management system that can be certified to ISO/IEC 20000, becomes a greater challenge; especially when the management systems have to be integrated to achieve the most cost-effective and efficient corporate structure.

IT Governance expert consultants can help you measure whether your IT services are adding real value to your business. We have substantial real-world experience as a professional services company specialising in IT GRC-related management systems. Our consulting team can help you to design and deploy IT service management structures, such as ITIL® and ISO20000, and integrate them with other systems, such as ISO/IEC 27001, ISO22301, ISO14001 and COBIT®.

For more information about IT Governance consultancy for IT service management, see:

http://www.itgovernance.co.uk/itsm-itil-iso20000-consultancy.aspx.

Newsletter

IT governance is one of the hottest topics in business today, not least because it is also the fastest moving, so what better way to keep up than by subscribing to ITG's free monthly newsletter *Sentinel*? It provides monthly updates and resources across the whole spectrum of IT governance subject matter, including risk management, information security, ITIL and IT service management, project governance, compliance and so much more. Subscribe for your free copy at: *www.itgovernance.co.uk/newsletter.aspx*.